AMERICAN WESTERN ART

AMERICAN WESTERN ART

THE ROCKWELL MUSEUM

Special thanks to the following for
their contributions to the catalogue:

Bob and Hertha Rockwell
Deborah J. Fero
Karen N. DePonceau Flint
Nancy W. Gardner
Robyn G. Peterson
P. Jensen Monroe
Mercedes C. Skidmore

and to Corning Glass Works for its
continued support of The Rockwell Museum.

ISBN 0-9622038-1-5
Library of Congress Catalogue Card No. 89-060295
The Rockwell Museum
Cedar Street at Denison Parkway
Corning, New York 14830
(607) 937-5386

Designed by Mary Lou Littrell
Printed by Village Craftsmen
Princeton Polychrome Press
Photography by James O. Milmoe,
Nicholas L. Williams, and Charles W. Swain

COLLECTING WESTERN ART

MOST PEOPLE ARE COLLECTORS to some degree, but few are fortunate enough to collect objects that have value to others and finally end up in a museum. When Hertha and I began buying American western art in the early 1960s, our purpose was to fill our home with the things we loved. At the time we had no idea that there would one day be The Rockwell Museum in our hometown of Corning. As fate would have it, some luck, our love of the West and collecting, a lot of encouragement from great friends in the field, and the faith and financial support of a community and a corporation converged to make it happen.

I was born a collector. As a boy growing up in Colorado, I collected bugs and butterflies, coins and stamps, arrowheads, animal skulls, traps (from mouse traps to grizzly bear traps) – even petrified wood and dinosaur bones. It was in my blood: a love of collecting and a love of the West. However, it wasn't until Hertha and I were in our fifties, living in Corning, New York, that we started collecting paintings and bronzes, as well as Carder Steuben glass and turn-of-the-century toys, which were our other loves.

Now comes the luck. The 1960s couldn't have been a better time for us to begin buying western art. The great collectors such as Amon Carter and Thomas Gilcrease had already put their collections together and we were the only serious collectors at that time. A collector doesn't often say he's lucky when his first acquisition turns out to be a fake, but I can say that now. Because a "Remington" painting that I bought in Elmira was not authentic, I became determined to learn all I could from the experts and to collect in earnest.

A fine collection cannot be assembled without the help of knowledgeable people – and it helps when they are friends. Dr. Harold McCracken, former director of the Whitney Gallery of Western Art in Cody, Wyoming, was our main advisor on reliable dealers. One was Jack Bartfield who was a great friend and the source for many of our finest acquisitions. Another was Rudolph Wunderlich from whom we bought many of our Remingtons. Others like Leo and Tony Lombardo and Helen Card found fine works by many of the western illustrators for us.

I could write a book about Fred Renner. He was the definitive expert on C. M. Russell and it was through him that we acquired most of our Russells, including my favorite picture, "A Mix Up." I first met Fred when he came to Corning in 1962 to make a record of our Russells. His second wife, Ginger, shares Fred's love of Russell, and continues his work on Russell's life and work. Her book, *The Limitless Sky*, is not only an account of Russell's life but is a catalogue of the Museum's Russell collection.

Many of the great contemporary western artists are our friends too. Among those whose paintings we purchased were Nick Eggenhofer, Bob Lougheed, and Charlie Dye – men who have now "passed over the great divide."

When our collection outgrew our home, we moved much of the art to our department store, making it a gallery of sorts. In 1965, about 50 of the finest works went on loan to the National Cowboy Hall of Fame in Oklahoma City, which had no permanent collection when it opened.

Other museums were interested in the western art, but our hope was that the three collections could stay together in Corning. Thanks to the efforts of James Houghton and Thomas Buechner of Corning Glass Works, the Company pledged its support to create and aid in financing the operation of a permanent home in Corning for the western art, Carder Steuben glass, and toys.

Hertha and I will never be able to express adequately our appreciation to Corning Glass Works for its contributions and interest that continue to this day. The Rockwell Museum would not exist, and the objects that we collected with care and love 28 years ago would be facing an uncertain future, if it were not for this support.

Robert F. Rockwell, Jr.
Founding Collector

INTRODUCTION

IN A FIELD AS DIVERSE AS American western art, it is rare to find a collection that expresses as consistent a vision as does The Rockwell Museum's. In large part, this is due to the fact that the core of a collection of paintings, sculpture, and works on paper, executed in a representational style, was assembled by one western art enthusiast, Robert F. Rockwell, Jr. Over time, the collection has been augmented by many individuals who recognize and are inspired by Mr. Rockwell's desire to continue a tradition established by artists from Catlin to Remington: that of bringing the romance and excitement of the West to audiences in the East.

The visitor to The Rockwell Museum will be treated to a walk through time, from the narrative works by the explorer-artists of the early nineteenth century to the nostalgic creations of twentieth-century artists. The visitor travels from Joseph Henry Sharp's New Mexico past Albert Bierstadt's Rocky Mountains to Charles M. Russell's Montana. He or she will see stark, documentary realism as well as romantic overstatements of history for which western art is so justly famous. In short, the visitor will share the artists' glimpses into the heartland of North America.

The Rockwell Museum's collection includes works by many familiar artists. We are particularly fortunate in our holdings of paintings by George Catlin, Alfred Jacob Miller, Seth Eastman, and John Mix Stanley who visited the land beyond the Mississippi River in the early 1800s to document a primitive Eden and its exotic inhabitants. Both Frederic Remington and Russell, the great masters, are well represented. Indeed, two volumes of Francis Parkman's *The Oregon Trail,* with original watercolor illustrations by Russell, are perhaps the Museum's greatest treasures. There are a number of exceptionally fine paintings by the founders of the Taos Society of Artists, Sharp and E. Irving Couse. Other highlights include a wide range of work by the big-game painter Carl Rungius and a number of etchings by the California artist Edward Borein.

This catalogue has been designed from the first to serve a dual purpose, for not only did we plan to meet the needs of scholars unacquainted with the scope and strengths of our collection, we wanted to satisfy our visitors who desire to take away from the Museum a bit more than memories of its western art. We hope that we have succeeded.

Arthur C. Townsend
Director

GEORGE CATLIN

(1796 – 1872)
b. Wilkes-Barre, Pennsylvania

"Black and blue cloth and civilization are destined, not only to veil, but to obliterate the grace and beauty of Nature. Man, in the simplicity and loftiness of his nature, unrestrained and unfettered by the disguises of art, is surely the most beautiful model for the painter, – and the country from which he hails is unquestionably the best study or school of the arts in the world: such I am sure, from the models I have seen, is the wilderness of North America. And the history and customs of such a people, preserved by pictorial illustrations, are themes worthy of the life-time of one man, and nothing short of the loss of my life shall prevent me from visiting their country and of becoming their historian."

Plate 1.
Breaking Down the Wild Horse,
Oil on canvas, 26″ x 32″, ca. 1840,
Bequest of Clara S. Peck.

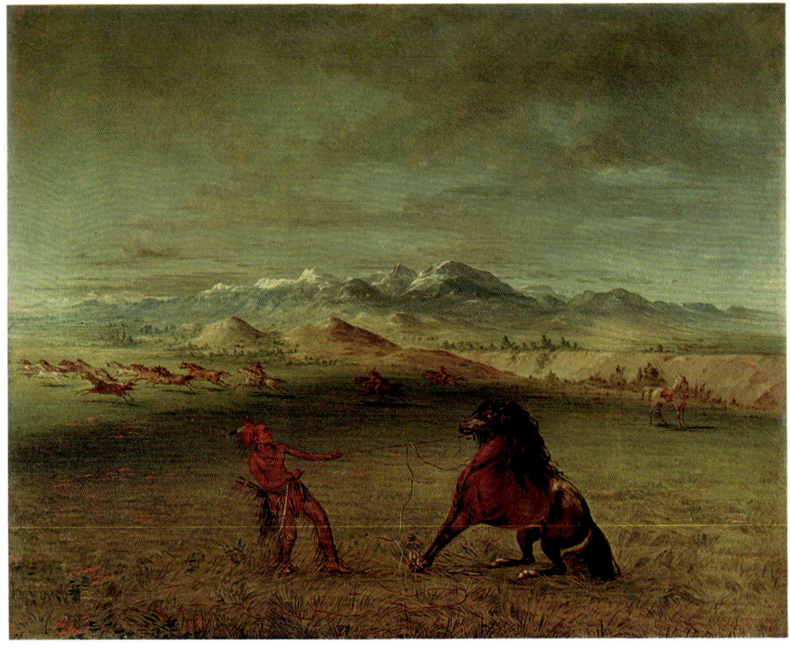

Plate 2. *The Mandan Indians*, Oil on board, 18″ x 24⅜″, 1871.

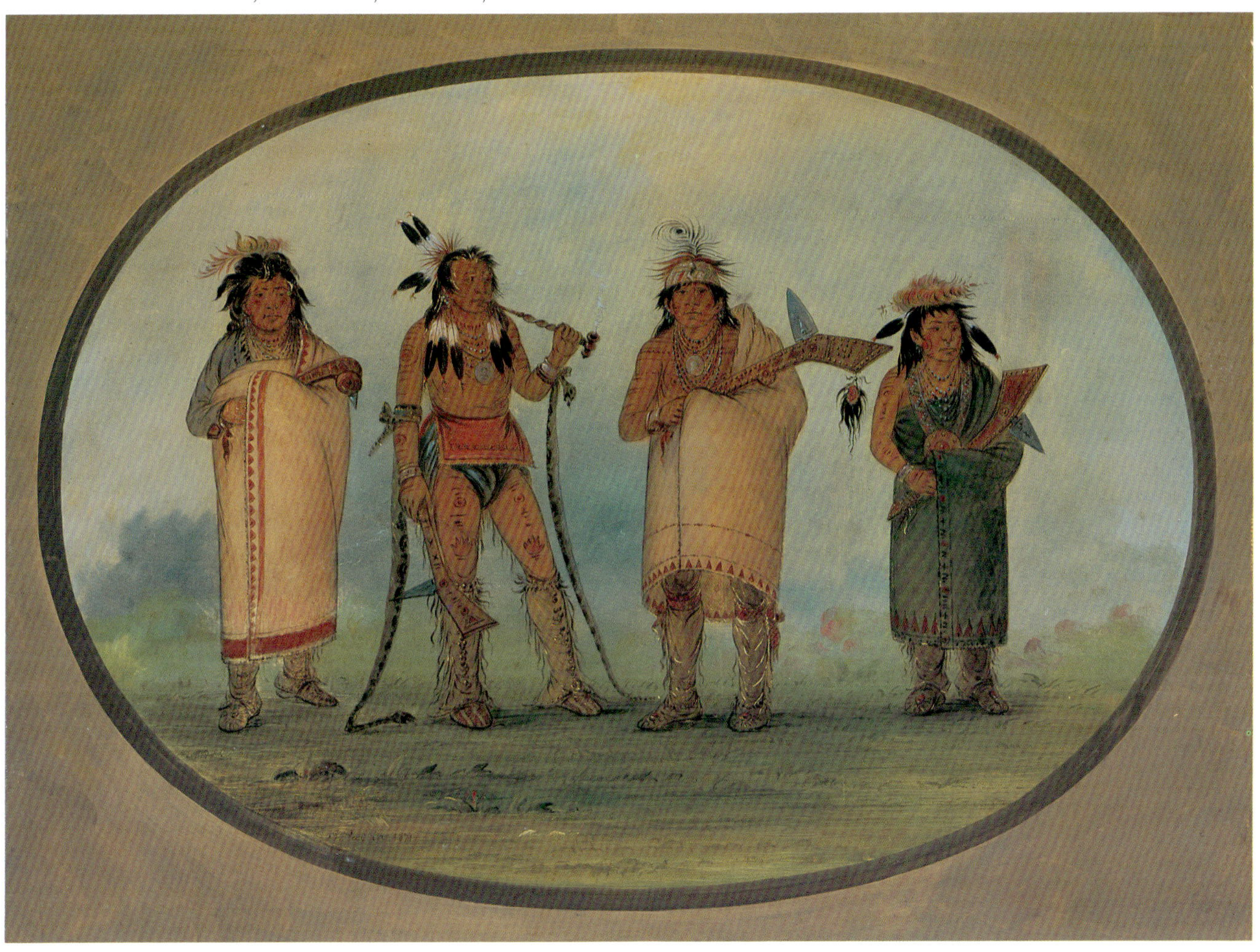

SETH EASTMAN

(1808 – 1875)
b. Brunswick, Maine

"His position and official status in the Indian country, and frequent contact with them, has enabled him to study minutely their character and peculiarities; and pursuing, for pleasure and amusement, the best of his tastes, he has been enabled to transfer to the canvas a more animated picture of real Indian life, than any we have ever seen before. Generally, the Indian is averse to having his portrait, or anything connected with him, painted. He believes it shortens his life. Capt. E. has had the opportunity to study his subject without these, or any other caprices, interfering with his purposes." – Missouri Record, *1847*

Plate 3. *The Tanner,* Oil on canvas, 30 3/16" x 25 1/4", 1848.

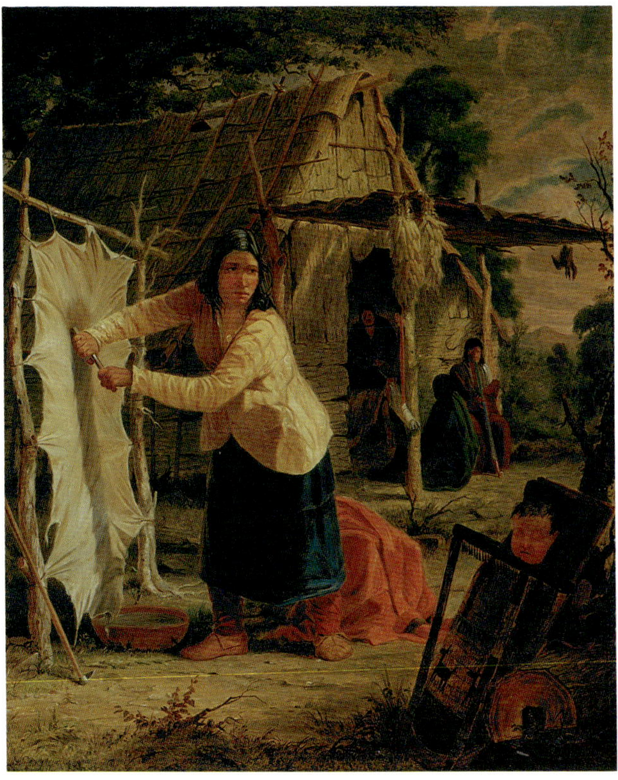

ALFRED JACOB MILLER

(1810 – 1874)
b. Baltimore, Maryland

. . . "for if you can weave such beautiful garlands with the simplest flowers of Nature – what a subject her wild sons of the West present, intermixed with their legendary history." – 1837

Plate 4.
Crow Chief on the Lookout,
Oil on canvas,
11⅝" x 9¾", sight, 1840,
Bequest of Clara S. Peck.

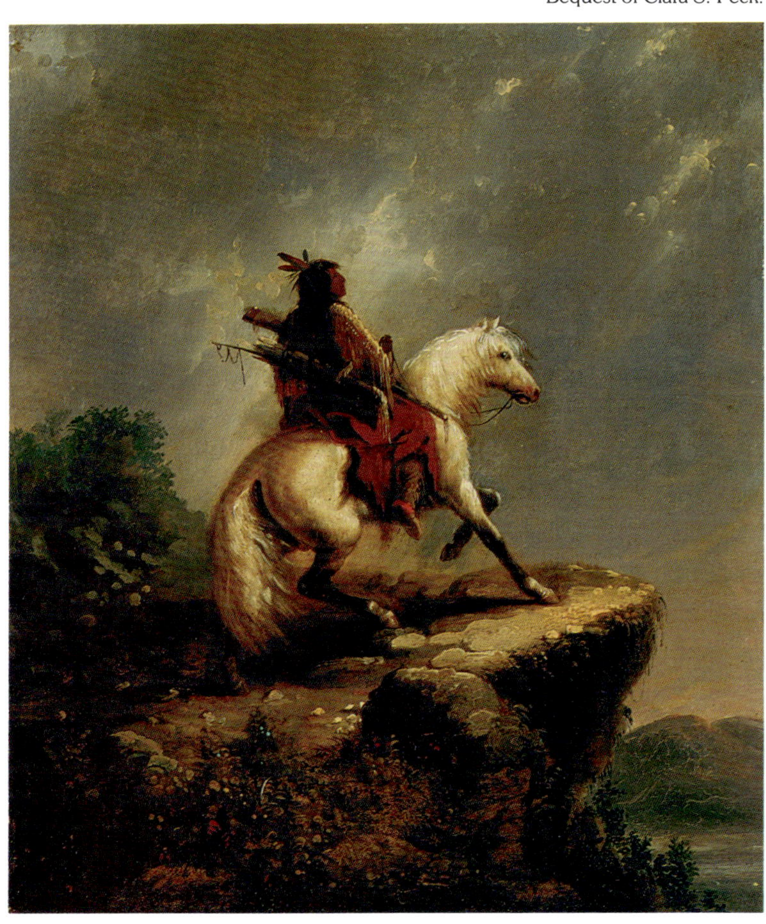

Plate 5. *Crow Indian on Horseback*, Oil on canvas, 19 3/16" x 25 3/8", sight, 1844, Bequest of Clara S. Peck.

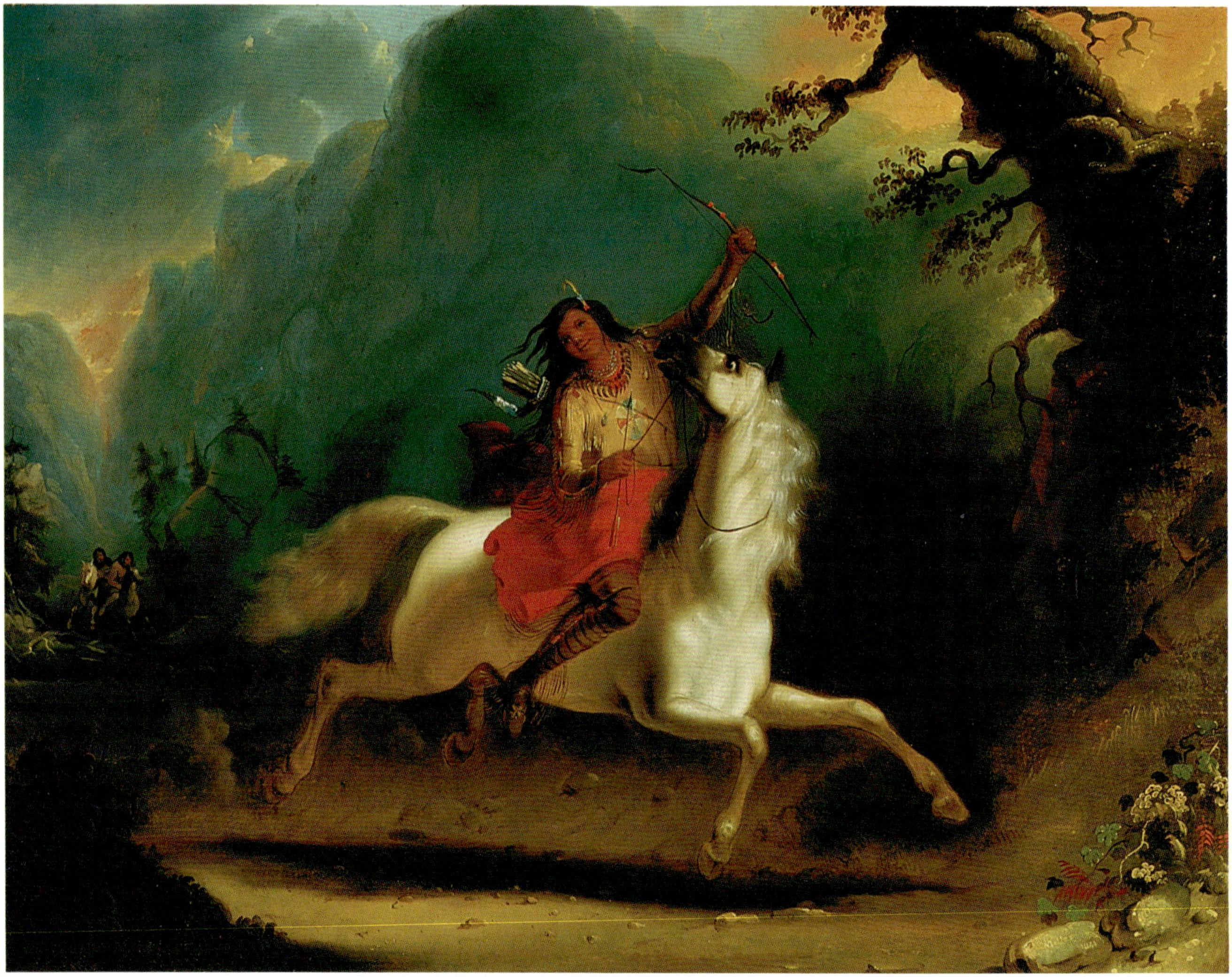

JOHN MIX STANLEY

(1814 – 1872)
b. Canandaigua, New York

"The first rays of the sun found us in the saddle prepared for a long march. But one day more remained for us to find the Piegan camp . . . At 1 o'clock I descended to a deep valley in which flows an affluent of Beaver river. Here was the Piegan camp, of ninety lodges, under the Chief Low Horn . . . Little Dog conducted me, with my party, to his lodge, and immediately the chiefs and braves collected in the 'Council Lodge,' to receive my message. The arrival of a 'pale face' was an unlooked for event, and hundreds followed me to the council, consisting of sixty of their principal men. The usual ceremony of smoking being concluded, I delivered my 'talk,' which was responded to by their chief saying, 'the whole camp would move at an early hour the following morning to council with the chief sent by their Great Father.' The day was spent in feasting with the several chiefs, all seeming to extend their hospitality; and while feasting with one chief, another had his messenger at the door of the lodge to conduct me to another."

Plate 6. *The Smoke Signal,* Oil on canvas, 29⅝" x 22½", sight, 1868.

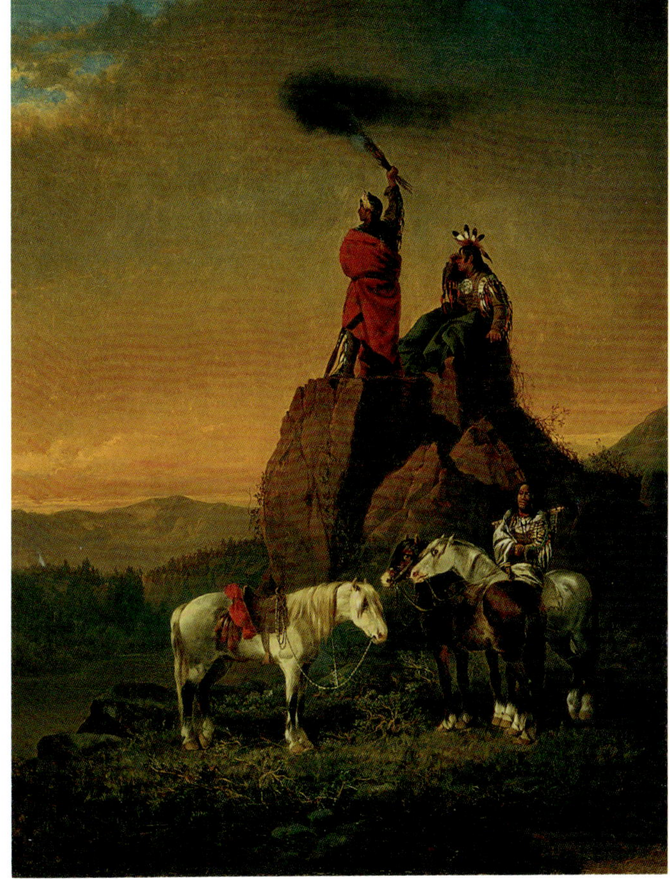

CORNELIUS DAVID KRIEGHOFF
(1815 – 1872)
b. Amsterdam, Holland

"Life is boring in the village but never in the woods."

Plate 7. *The Storyteller,* Oil on canvas, 13" x 18", 1855-1860, Gift of Clarence E. Gates.

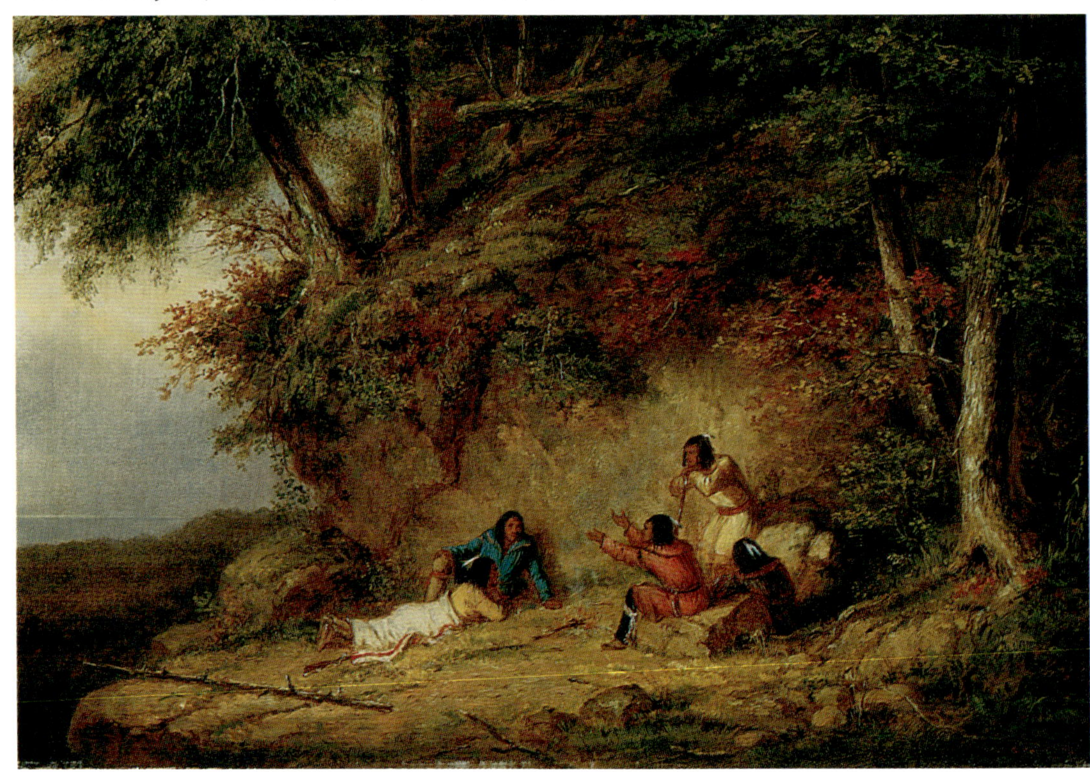

CARL (OR CHARLES) FERDINAND WIMAR
(1828 – 1862)
b. Siegburg, Germany

"If I last long enough, someday I shall be so rich that I can have a bank account."

Plate 8. *On the Warpath,* Oil on canvas, 6½" x 9⅜", sight, 1860, Bequest of Clara S. Peck.

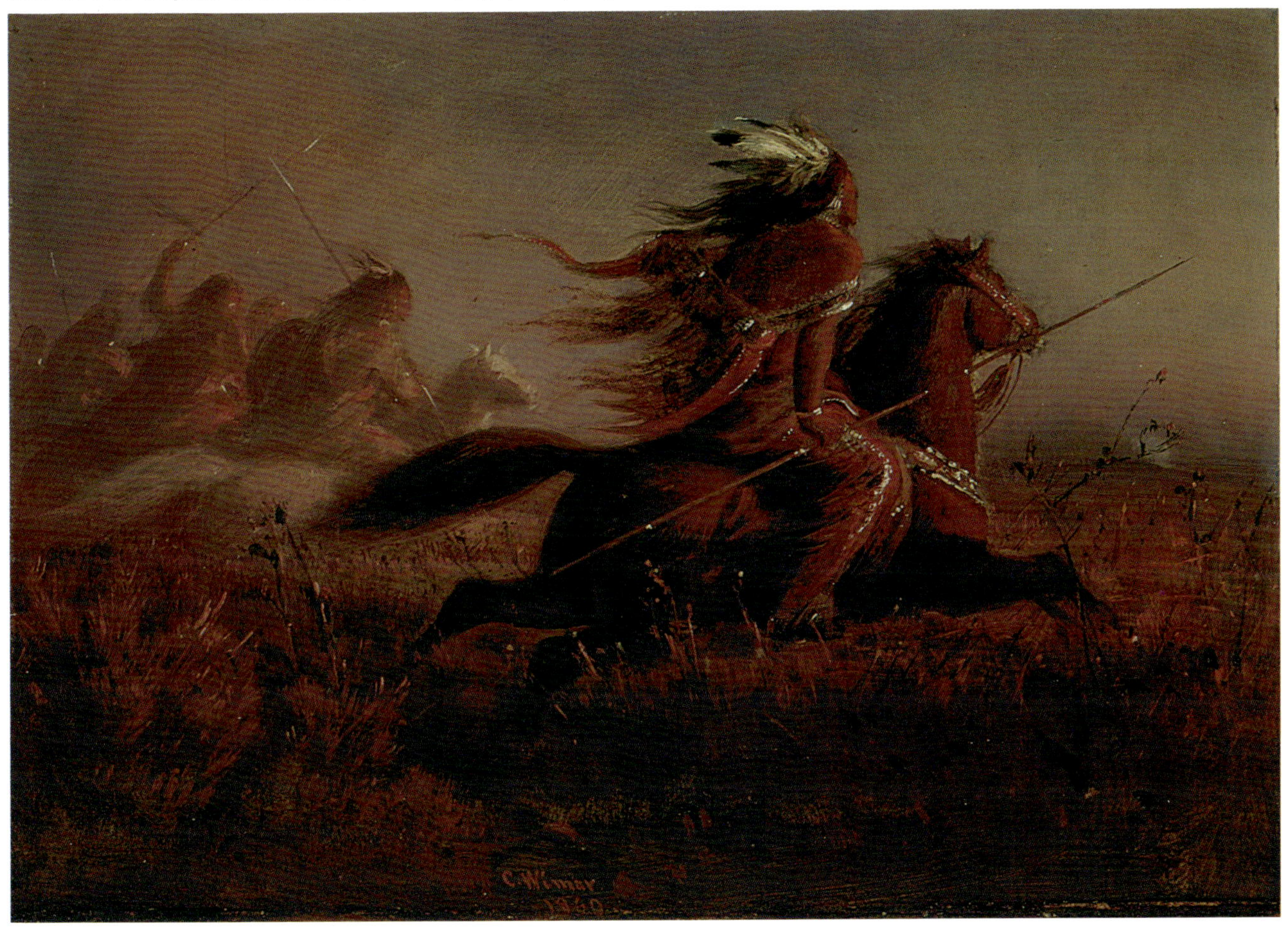

THOMAS HILL
(1829 – 1908)
b. Birmingham, England

"Accidental effects can only be gotten with a big brush, I depend entirely on accident – you have no idea how much is produced that way."

Plate 9. *Yosemite,* Oil on canvas, 35⅝″ x 29⅛″, n.d.

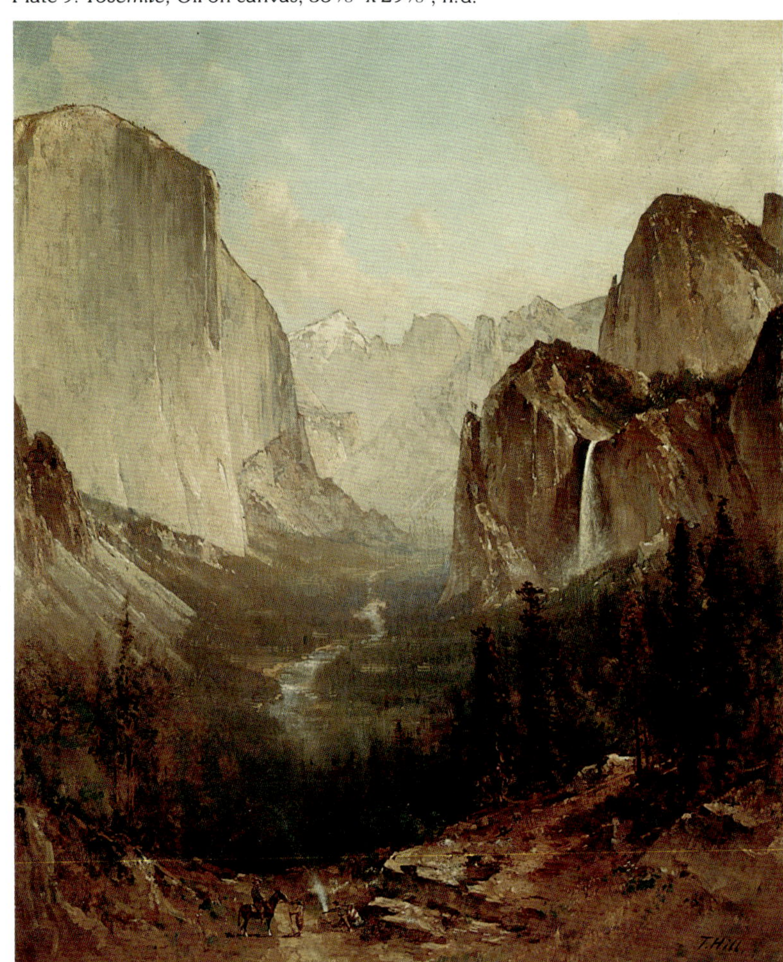

ALBERT BIERSTADT

(1830 – 1902)
b. Düsseldorf, Germany

"I am delighted with the scenery. The mountains are very fine; as seen from the plains, they resemble very much the Bernese Alps . . . The color of the mountains and of the plains, and, indeed, that of the entire country, reminds one of the color of Italy; in fact, we have here the Italy of America in a primitive condition."

– 1859

Plate 10. *Last of Fifty Million* or *Buffalo* or *Buffaloes Asleep*, Oil on canvas, 13⅜" x 18¼", ca. 1863, Collection of Robert F. Rockwell III.

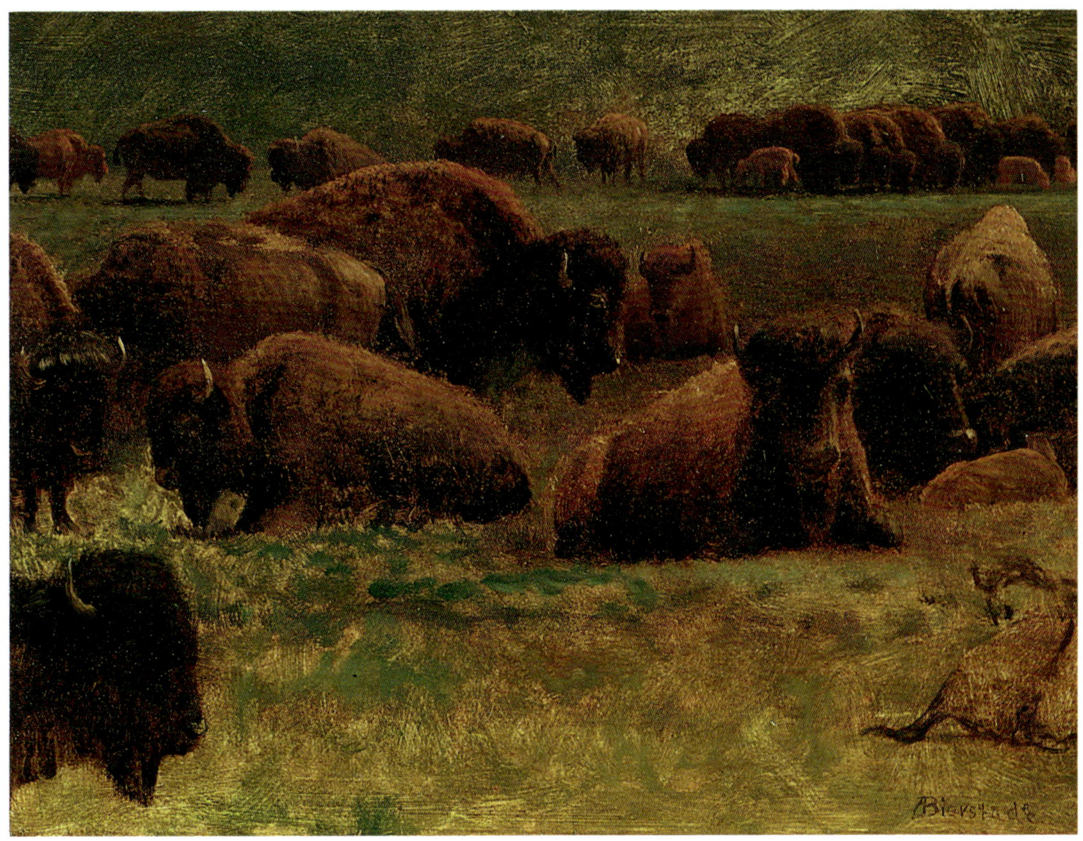

Plate 11. *Mt. Whitney,* Oil on canvas, 68⅞" x 116⅝", 1875.

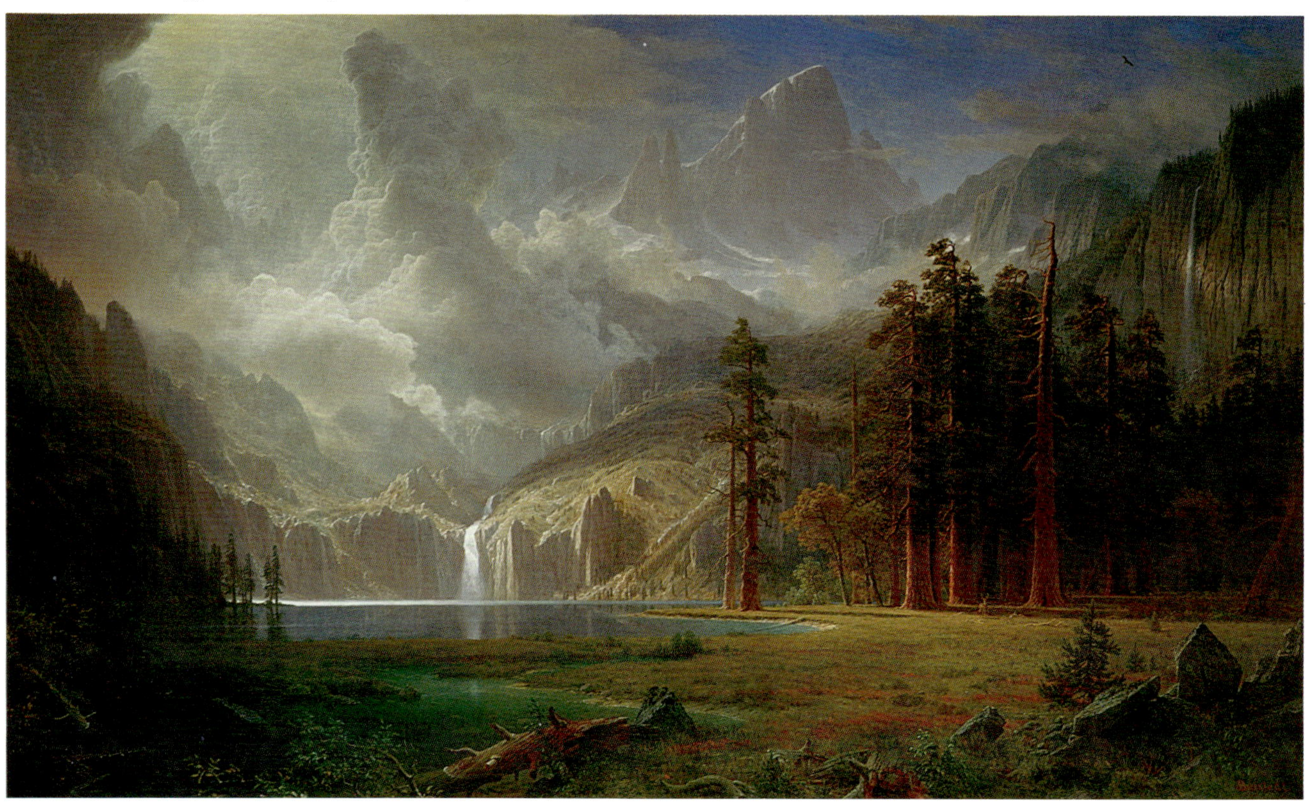

THOMAS MORAN

(1837 – 1926)
b. Bolton, Lancashire, England

"I place no value upon literal transcripts from Nature. My general scope is not realistic, all my tendencies are toward idealization . . . Topography in art is valueless . . . while I desired to tell truly of Nature, I did not wish to realize the scene literally, but to preserve and to convey its true impression."

Plate 12. *Crossing Green River,* Oil on canvas, 10″ x 16$\frac{11}{16}$″, 1877, Bequest of Clara S. Peck.

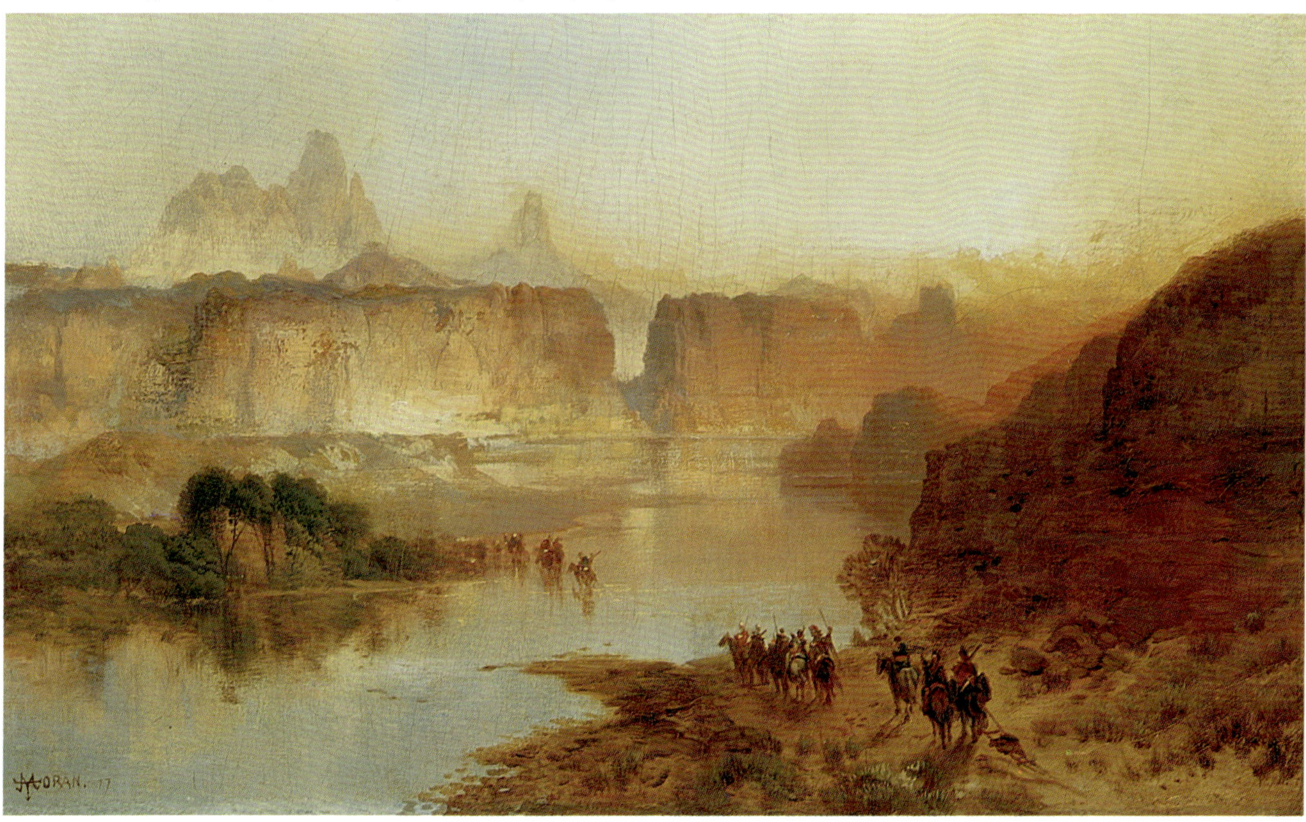

Plate 13. *Clouds in the Canyon,* Oil on canvas, 20″ x 25″, 1915.

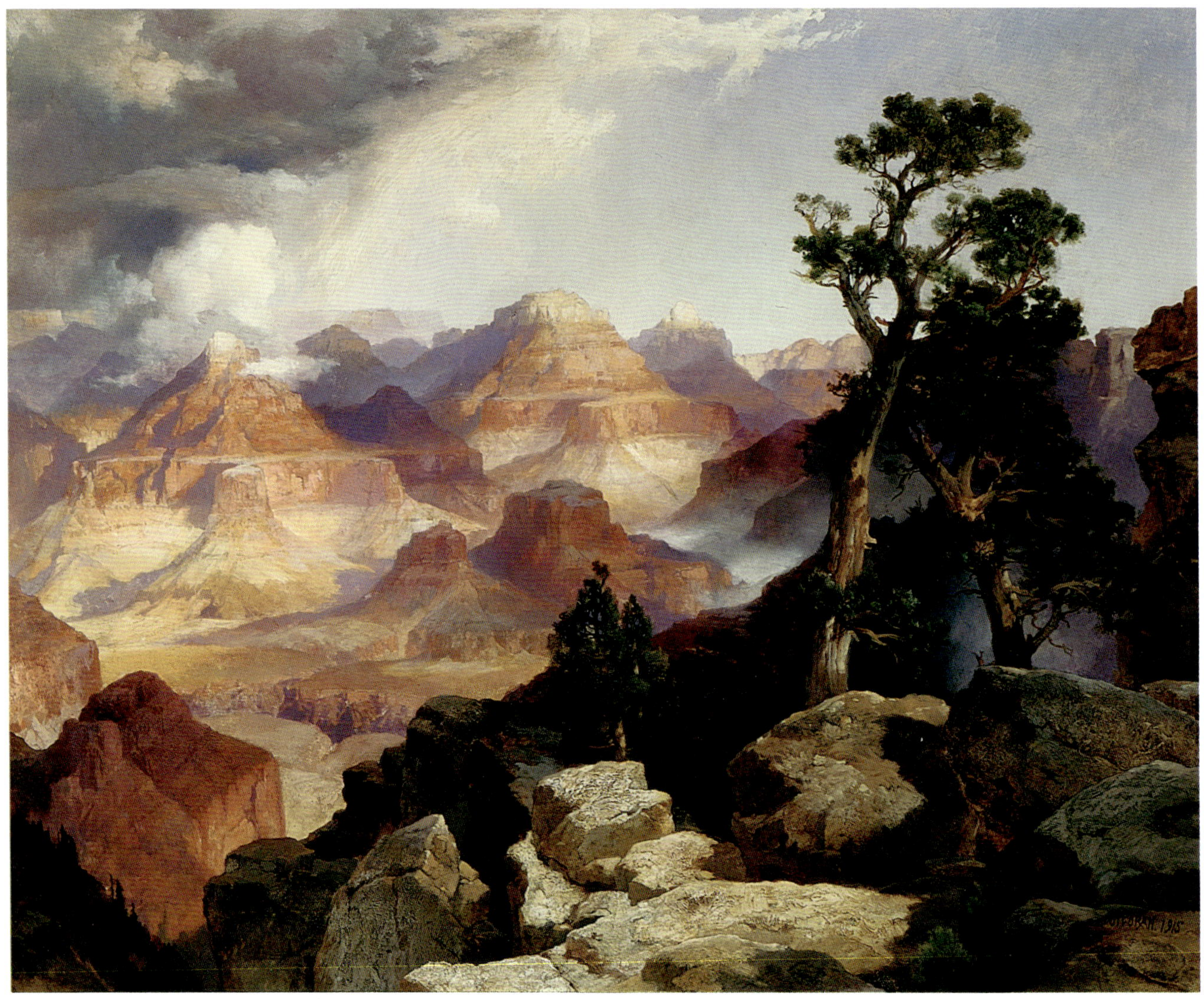

WILLIAM DE LA MONTAGNE CARY
(1840 – 1922)
b. Tappan, New York

"My pictures should appeal to the old timers. I have hundreds of pictures or sketches, in oil and pencil, with little memorandum [sic] on many of them but I failed to write their names on them." – 1919

Plate 14. *The Upper Missouri,* Oil on canvas, 14⅝" x 27⅜", sight, 1875. Collection of Robert F. Rockwell, Jr.

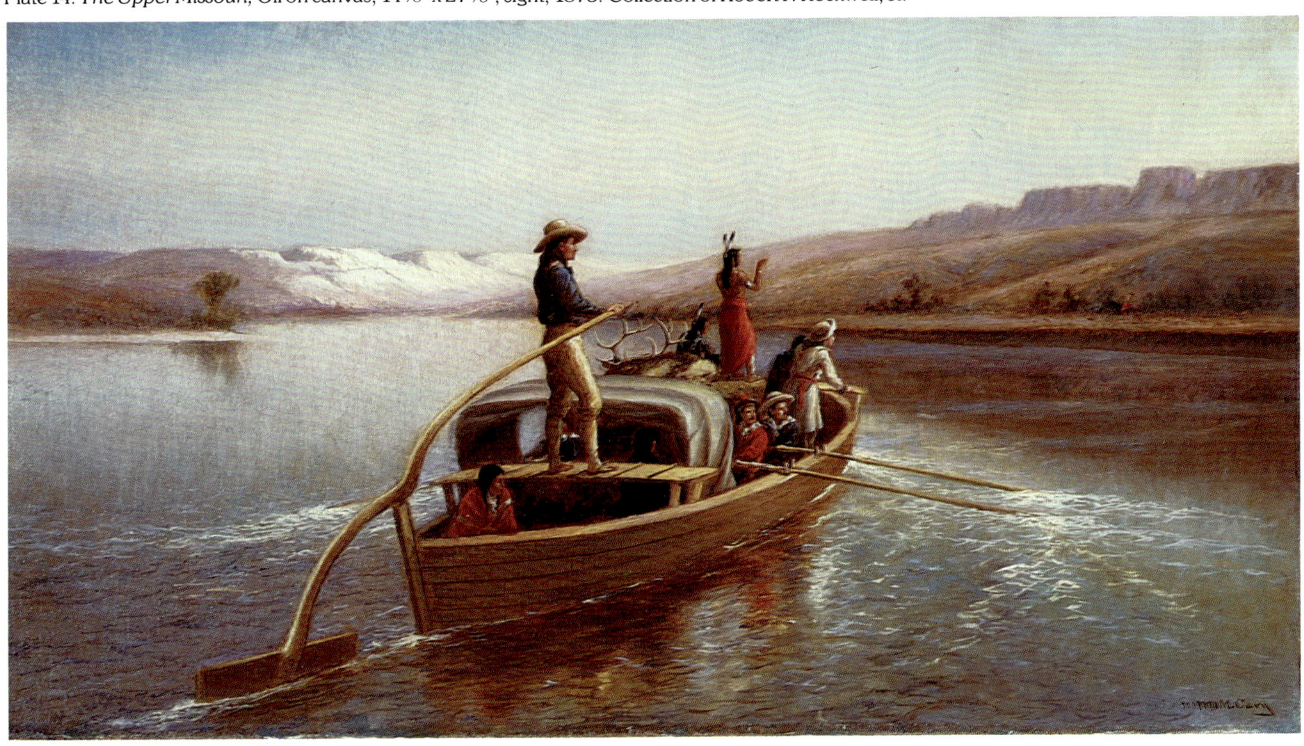

EDWARD KEMEYS

(1843 – 1907)
b. Savannah, Georgia

"I never killed a bird or animal but I posed it in various ways, illustrating endless motives in grouping. It was also my habit to skin and dissect continually after I had studied from the life, committing to memory almost, the forms and meaning of the anatomy of all these prairie creatures. Often to preserve some peculiar phase of expression, I posed the animal or bird upon a background of board, pinned it there while yet limber and let it stiffen. These studies were of incalculable value in teaching me the possibilities of anatomy and were lessons I never forgot. The groundwork was well laid, with no human teacher or guide, under the roof of no Art School but that of the sky and with no motive for so doing but the invisible Power which compelled me so to do. Why and wherefor [sic] I knew not till I came to my own. Then what a treasure house I found ready for use . . . What wonder then that I came to my birthright before I ever touched clay or realized the meaning of my happy task."

Plate 15. *Coyote,*
Bronze, 26" x 27" x 10½",
ca. 1900.

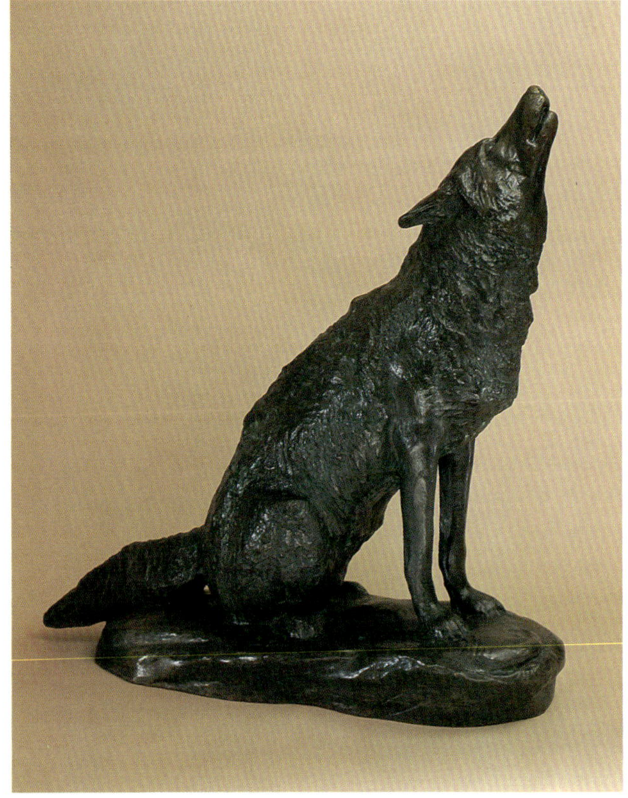

HENRY FRANÇOIS FARNY
(1847 – 1916)
b. Ribeauville, Alsace, France

"The plains, the buttes, the whole country, and its people are fuller of material for the artists than any other country in Europe."

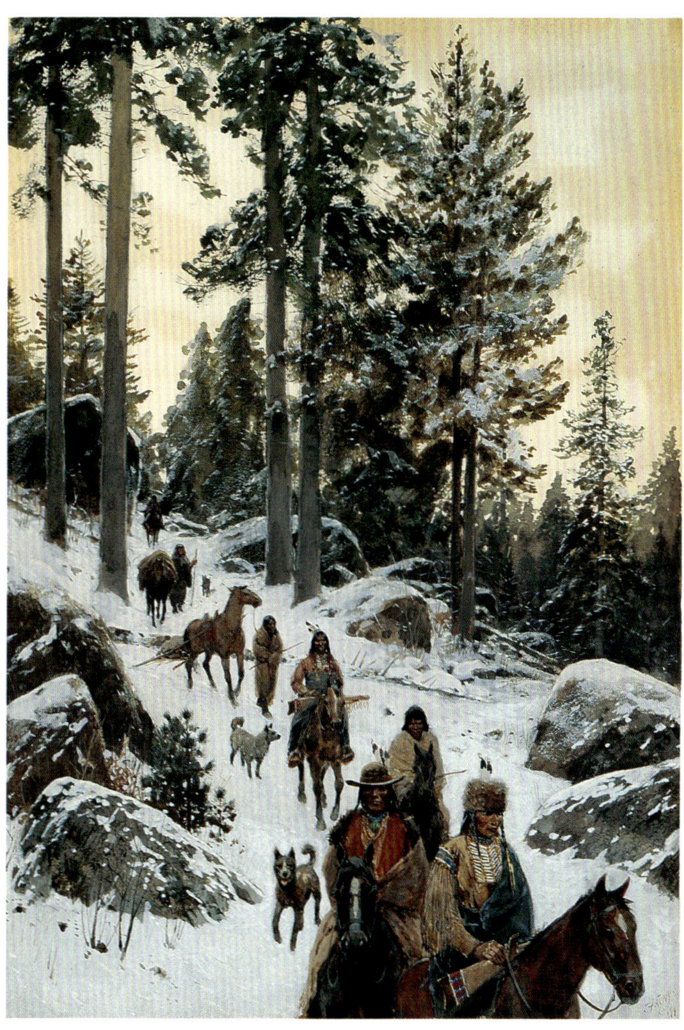

Plate 16.
On the Trail in Winter,
Gouache, 15¾" x 10⅞", sight,
1894.

Plate 17. *The Wailer,* Gouache, 9⅛″ x 14¾″, sight, 1895.

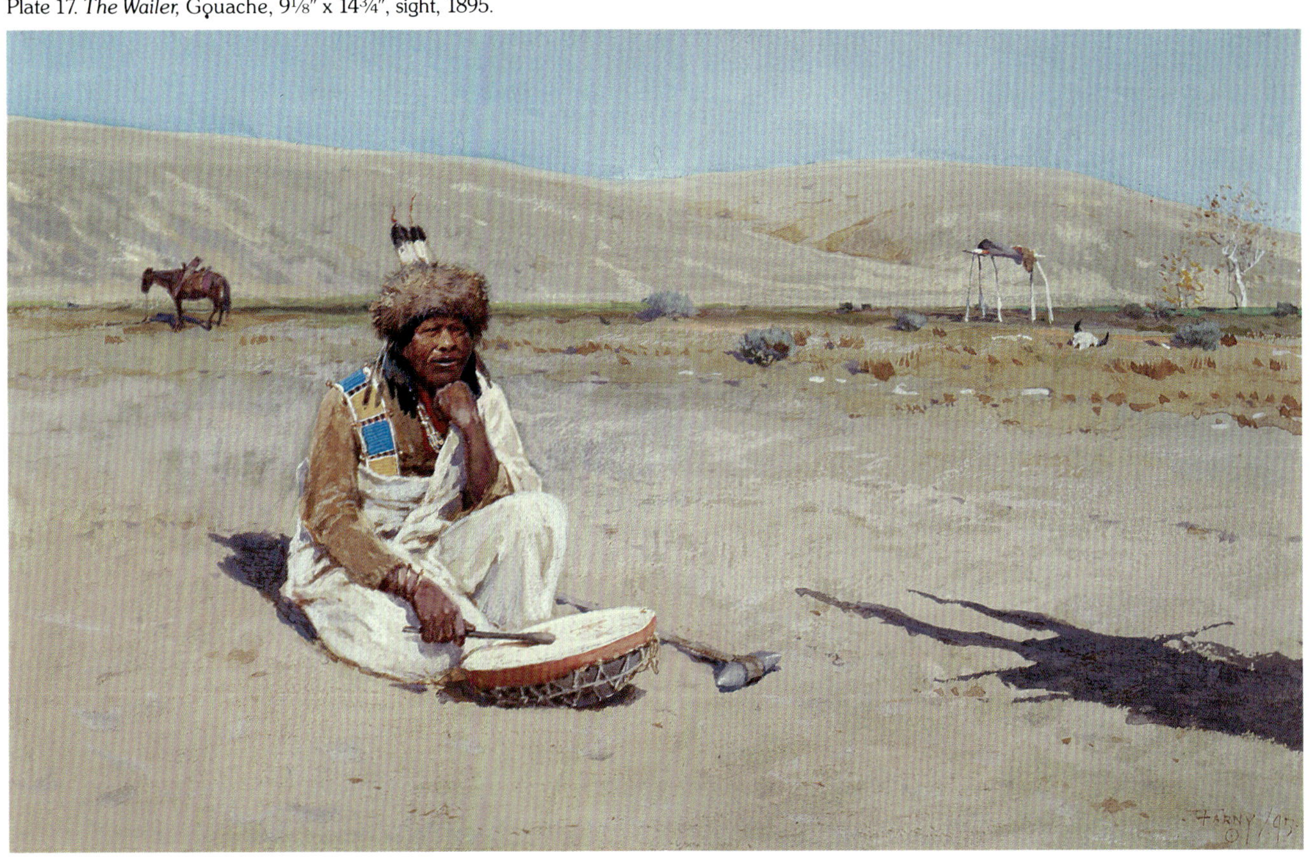

EDGAR SAMUEL PAXSON

(1852 – 1919)
b. East Hamburg, New York

"The iron heel of civilization has stamped out nations of men but it has never been able to wipe out pictures . . . Paxson was one of the men gifted to make them. I am a painter too but Paxson has done some things that I cannot do. He was a pioneer and a pioneer painter . . . Paxson loved Montana. May the land where he has gone be even more beautiful than the mountains that he loved." – C.M. Russell, 1919

Plate 18.
Heinmoot Tooyalaket, Chief Joseph of the Nez Perce,
Watercolor, 17½" x 12⅜", n.d.

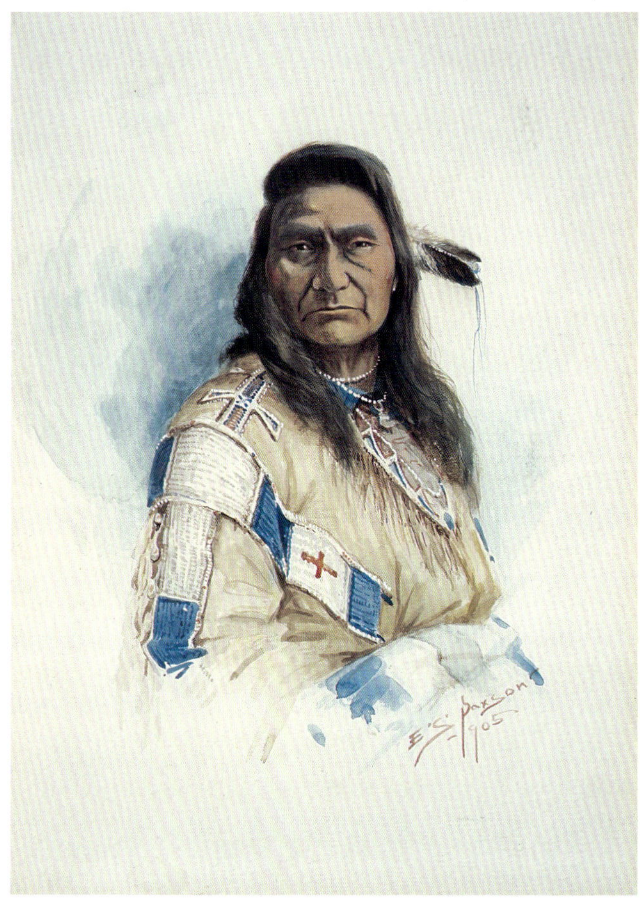

HERMAN WENDLEBORG HANSEN
(1854 – 1924)
b. Dithmarschen, Germany

"When I was last in Tucson there were four gambling houses running full blast night and day to every block. They were patronized by Indians, cowboys, sheepherders, niggars and Chinamen. Every man, whatever his color, wore a gun in sight, and I could walk up and down the main street of Tucson all day and every day of the week getting material for pictures, local color and new types. Now the town is killed from my point of view. I met a man here who had just come up from Arizona and he tells me they have shut down all the gambling houses tight, and not a gun in sight! Why the place hasn't the pictorial value of a copper cent any longer." – 1908

Plate 19.
Questionable Companions,
Watercolor, 19½″ x 29½″, sight,
ca. 1915.

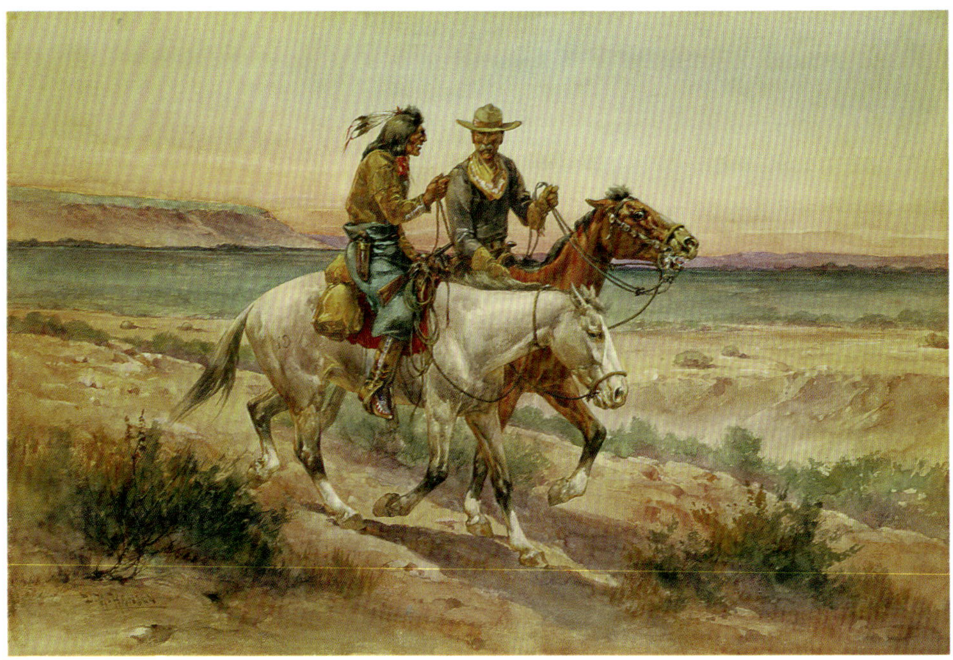

JOHN HAUSER
(1858 or 1859 – 1913)
b. Cincinnati, Ohio

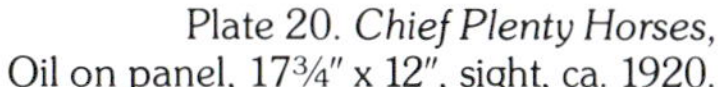

Plate 20. *Chief Plenty Horses,*
Oil on panel, 17¾″ x 12″, sight, ca. 1920.

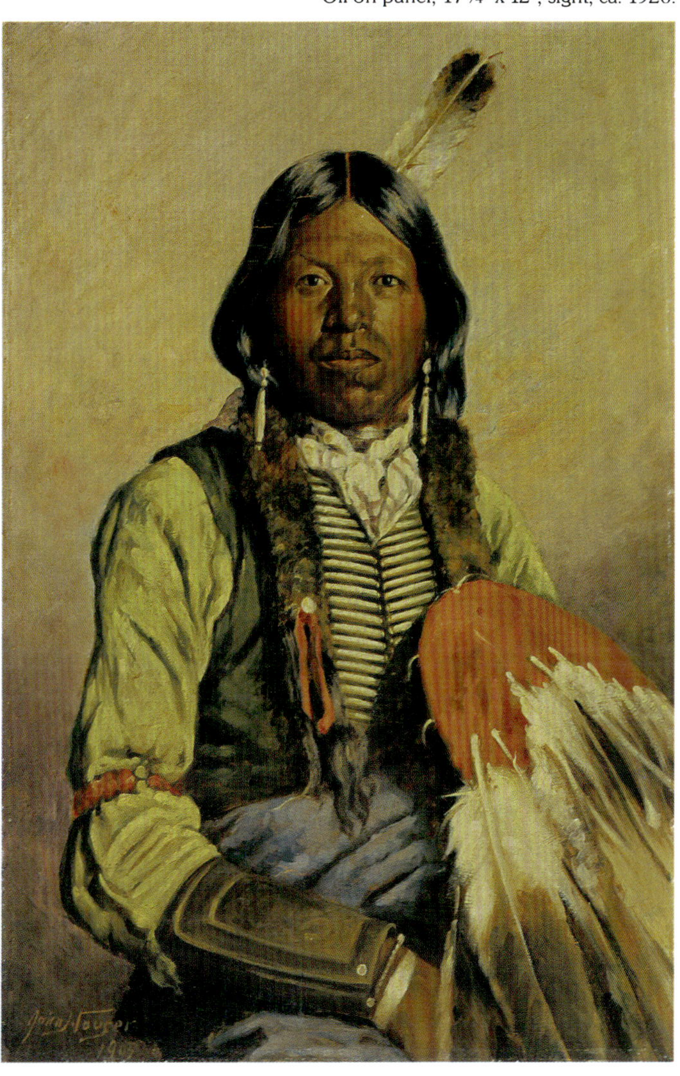

JOSEPH HENRY SHARP

(1859 – 1953)
b. Bridgeport, Ohio

"I was first attracted to the human side of the Indian; the character of the old warriors I found particularly interesting. Their romance and idealism are the most beautiful symbols brought down in the annals of time; their religion, their legends and superstitions are all unique. Not these alone, however, brought the greatest influence to bear on my work. It was the humanity of the present, the aspect we can see, know and feel that was my greatest aspiration."

Plate 21. *The Gift Dance Drummers*, Oil on canvas, 29½″ x 39½″, 1920.

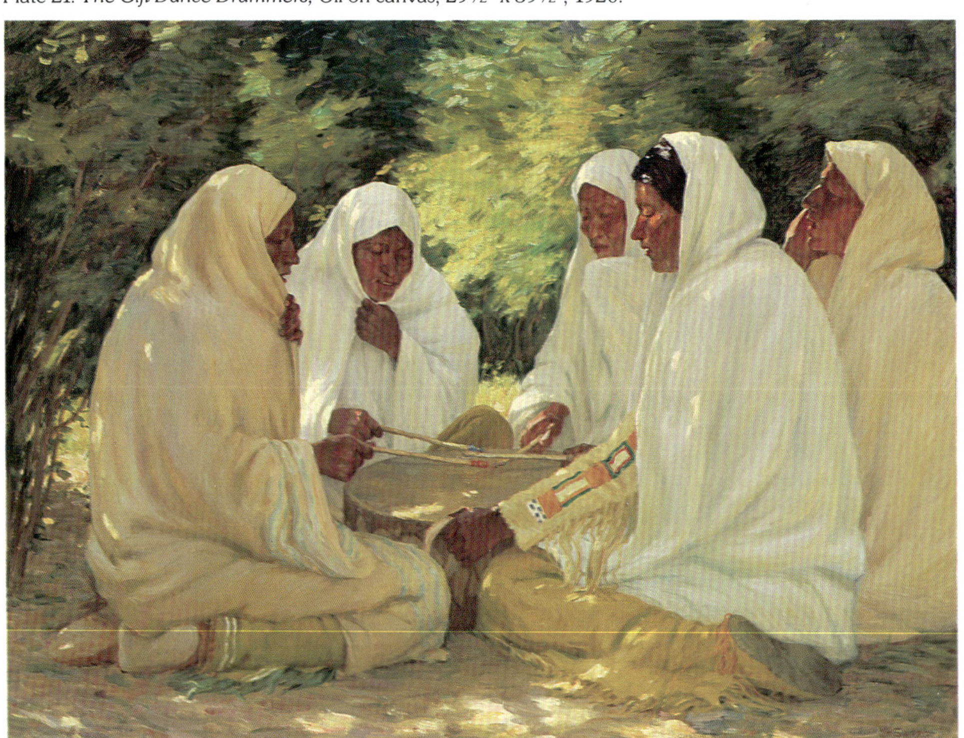

Plate 22. *Prayer to the Spirit of the Buffalo*, Oil on canvas, 29″ x 39″, 1910.

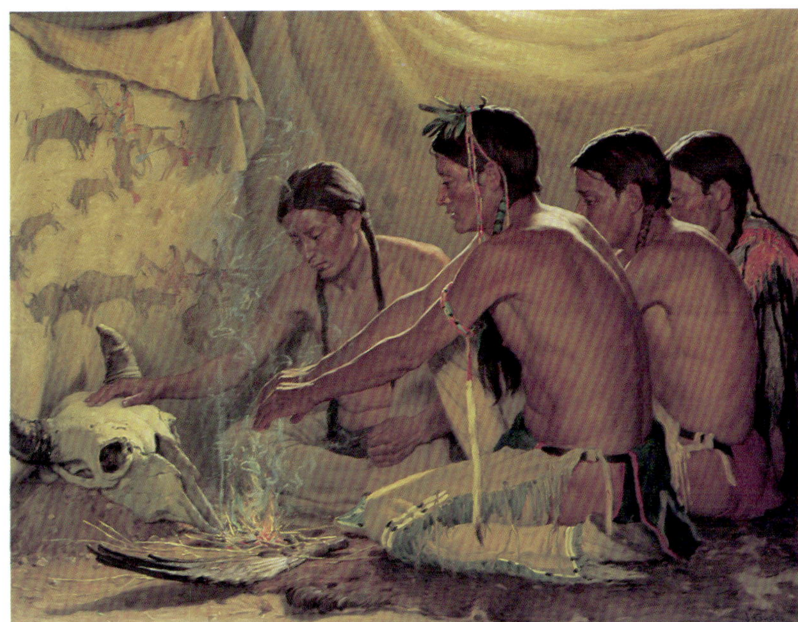

Plate 23. *Horse Runs Ahead, Sioux*,
Oil on canvas, 17½″ x 11¾″, 1910.

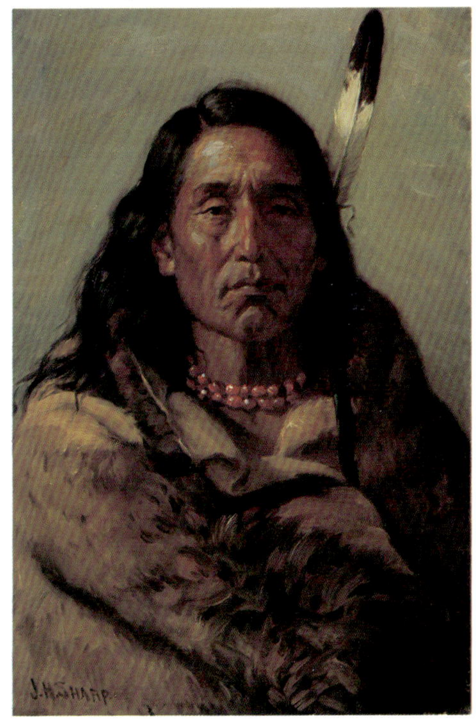

CHARLES SCHREYVOGEL

(1861 – 1912)
b. New York, New York

"I have not met any Fenimore Cooper Indians, although I have had the pleasure of knowing some good, honorable red men. The Indian is, as a rule, silent, stoical, and taciturn to a wonderful degree until he gets to know you."

Plate 24. *An Unexpected Enemy,* Oil on canvas, 33¾" x 24¾", sight, 1900.

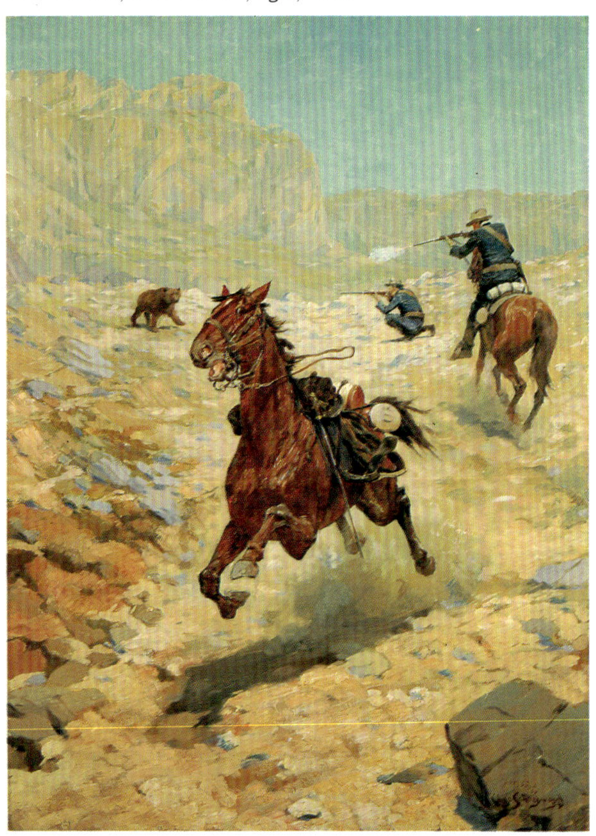

Plate 25. *The Last Drop,* Bronze, 13½" x 18", 1903.

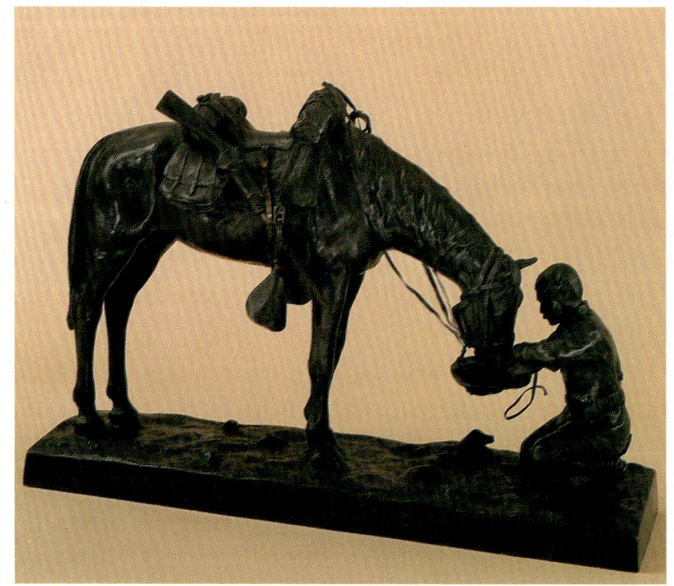

FREDERIC SACKRIDER REMINGTON

(1861 – 1909)
b. Canton, New York

"Youth is never appalled by the insistent demands of a great profession, because it is mostly unconscious of their existence. Time unfolds these abruptly enough. Art is a she-devil of a mistress, and, if at times in earlier days she would not even stoop to my way of thinking, I have persevered and will so continue. Some day, who knows, she may let me tell you some of my secrets. Meanwhile be patient, and if the recording of a day which is past infringes on the increasing interest of the present, be assured there are those who will set this down in turn and everything will be right in the end. Besides, artists must follow their own inclinations unreservedly. It's more a matter of heart than head, with nothing perfunctory about it. I saw the living, breathing end of three American centuries of smoke and dust and sweat, and I now see quite another thing where it all took place, but it does not appeal to me." – 1905

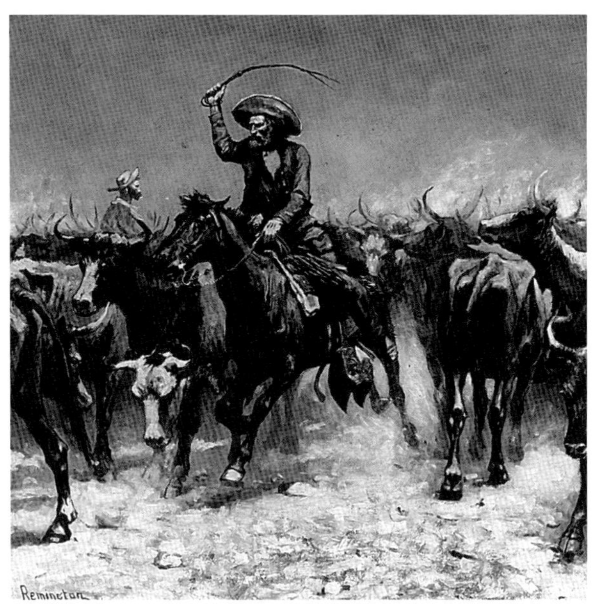

Plate 26. *Cutting Out a Steer,* Grisaille, 18" x 18", sight, 1888.

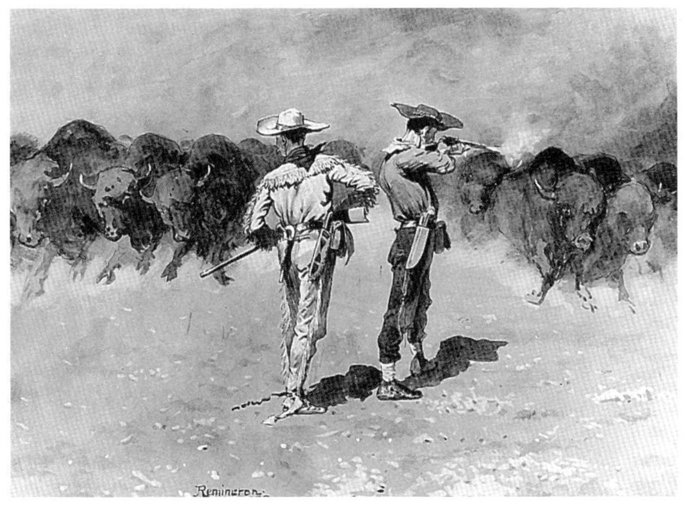

Plate 27. *Splitting the Herd,*
Gouache, 18" x 25¼", sight, 1889.

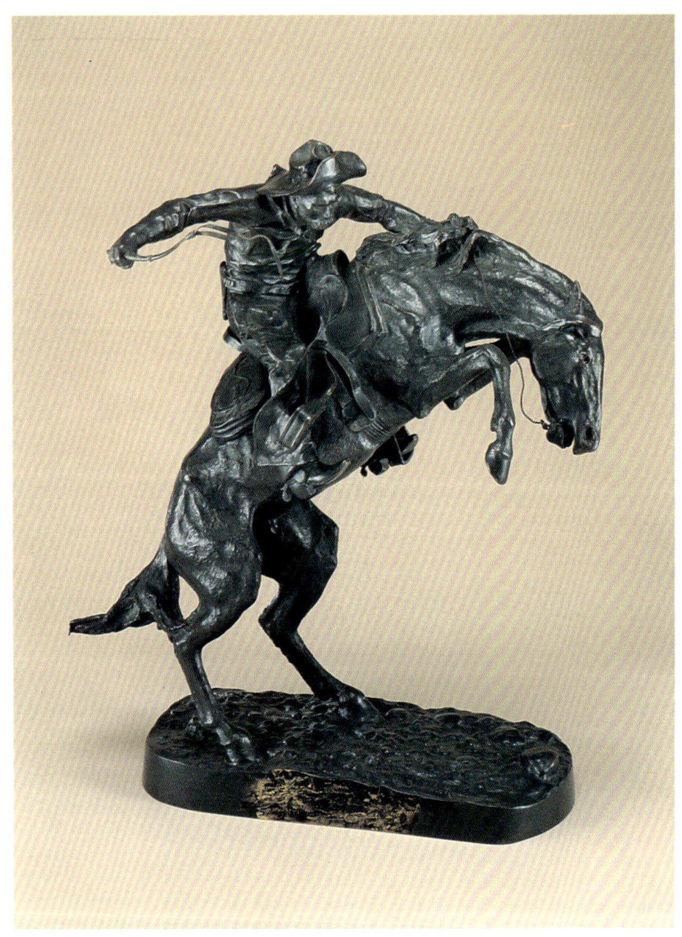

Plate 28. *Bronco Buster,* Bronze, 22 7/16″ x 21 7/8″ x 13 7/8″, 1895, Collection of Robert F. Rockwell, Jr.

Plate 29. *Lin McLean,* Ink and wash drawing, 15 3/8″ x 9 1/4″, 1897.

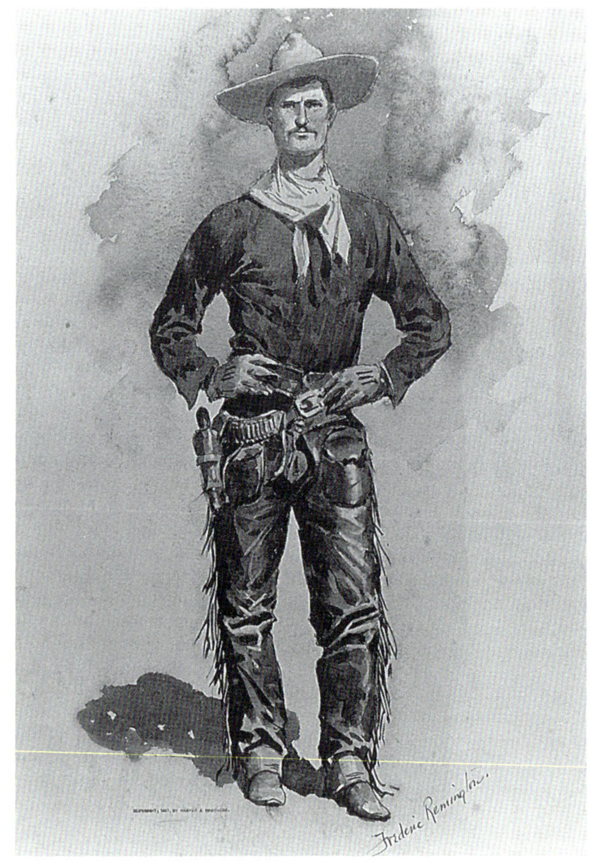

Plate 30. *Then I jumped to my feet and told the visitors to throw off their blankets,* Grisaille, 27″ x 40″, 1900.

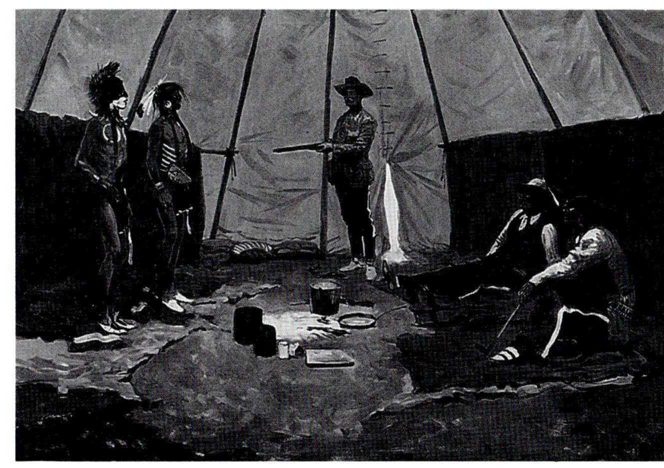

Plate 31. *The Arizona Cowboy,* Pastel and pencil drawing, $29\frac{7}{8}$″ x 26″, 1901.

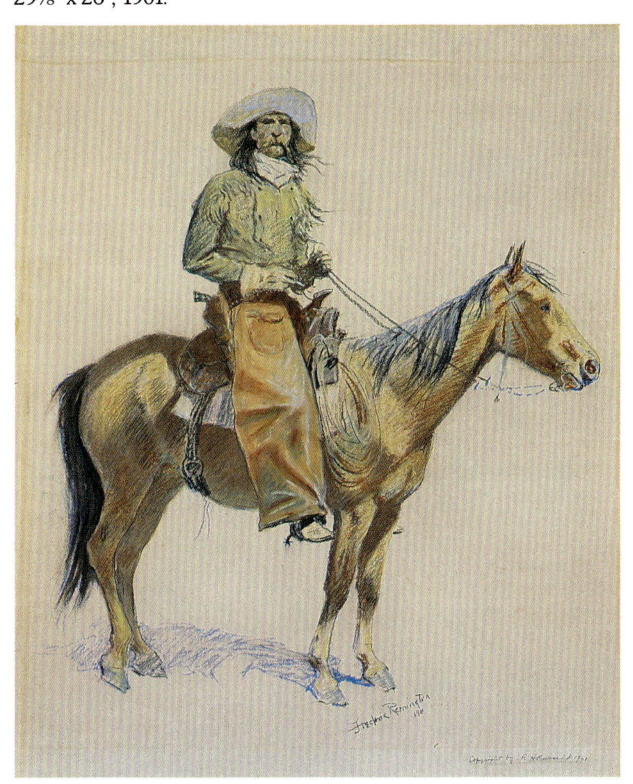

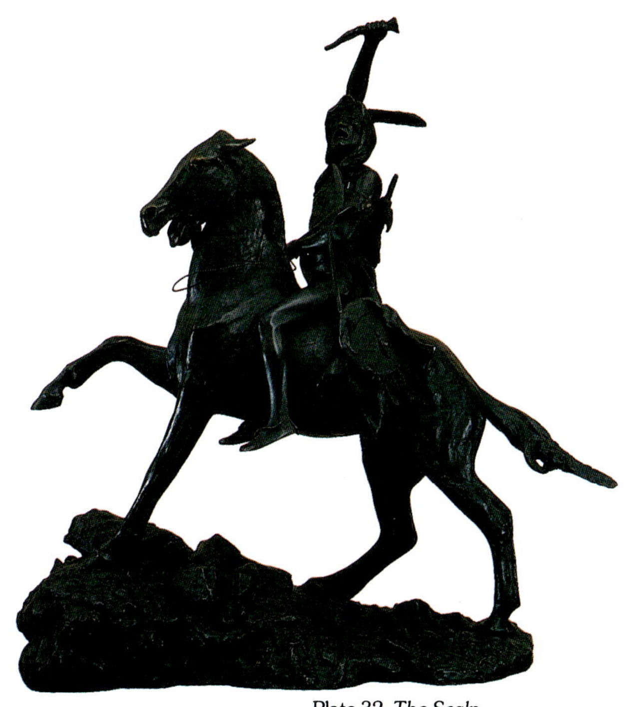

Plate 32. *The Scalp,* Bronze, $23\frac{1}{8}$″ x $22\frac{3}{16}$″ x 9″, 1901.

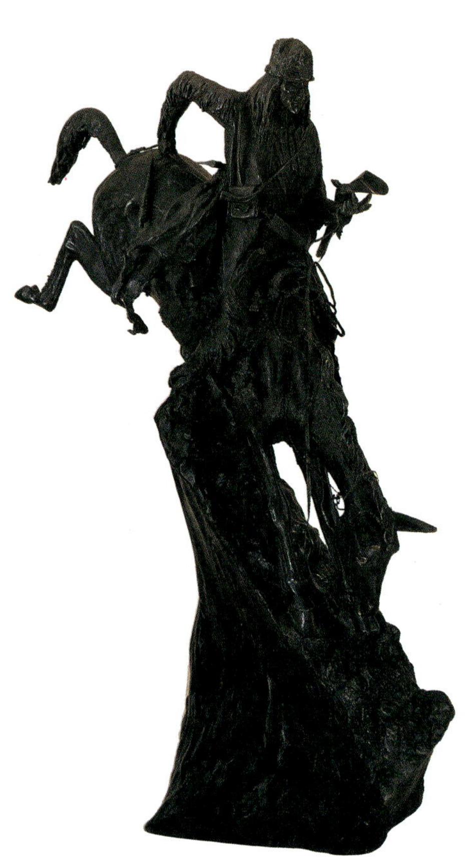

Plate 33. *The Mountain Man,*
Bronze, 28″ x 21½″ x 11″,
1903.

Plate 34. *The Rattlesnake,*
Bronze, 24″ x 18½″ x 11½″,
1905.

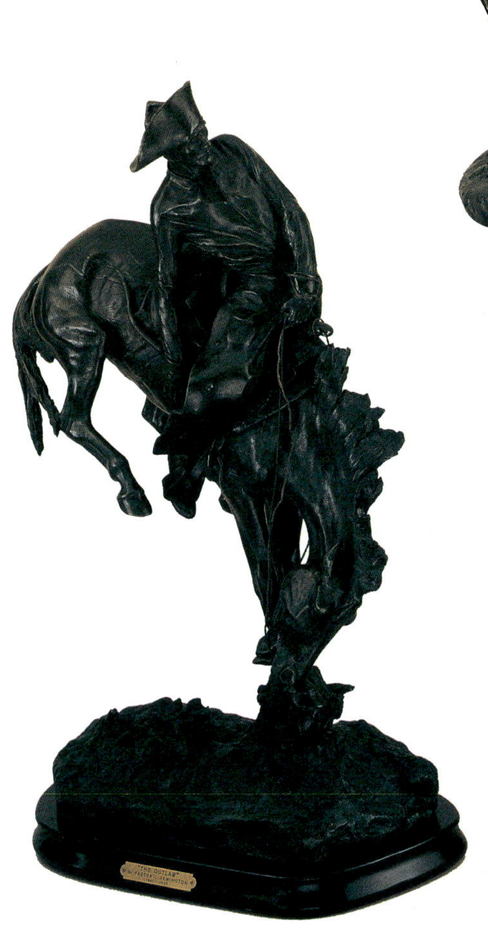

Plate 35. *The Outlaw,*
Bronze, 25¾″ x 13½″ x 10″,
1906.

Plate 36. *Winter Campaign,* Oil on canvas, 27″ x 40⅛″, 1909.

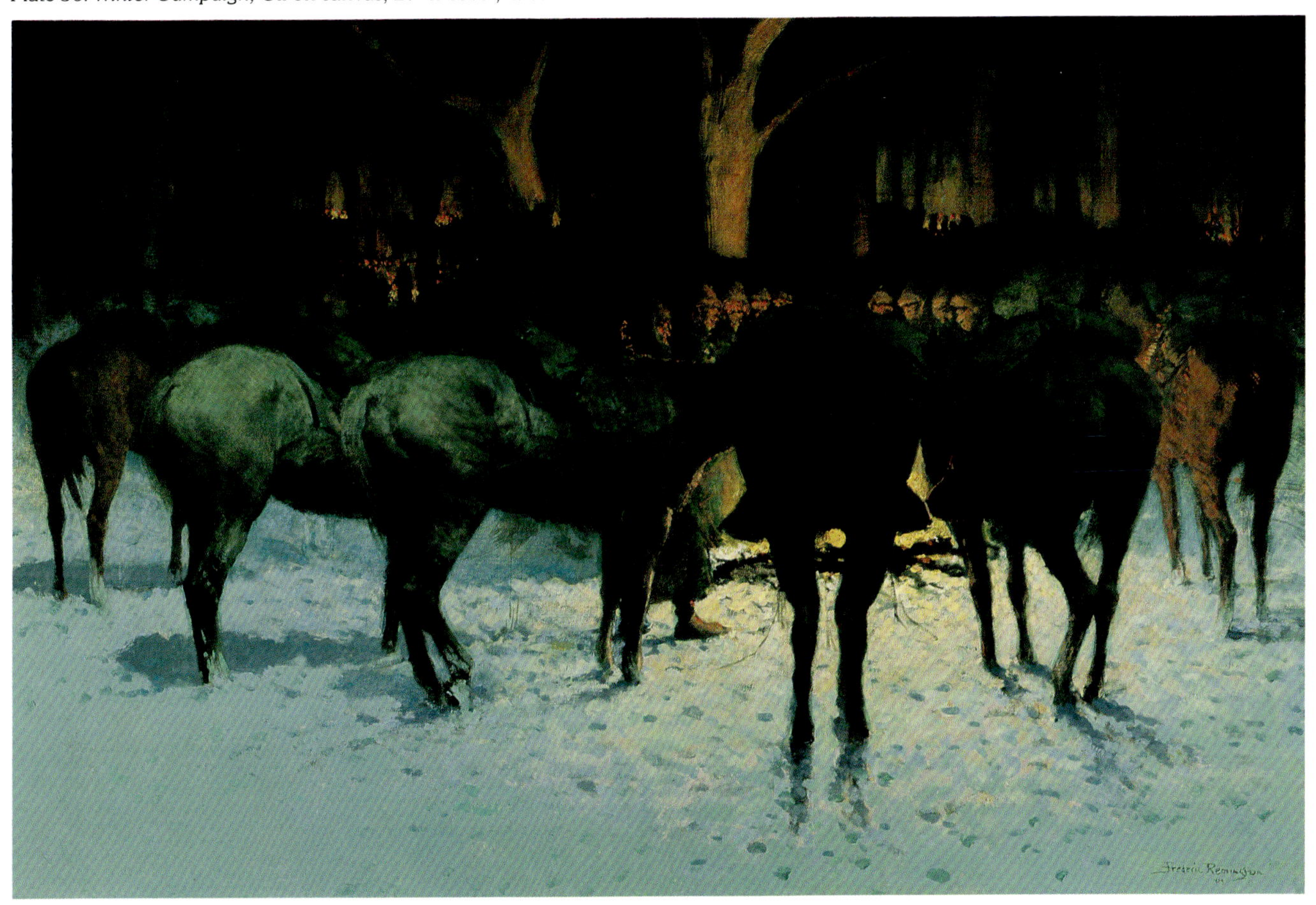

CHARLES MARION RUSSELL

(1864–1926)
b. St. Louis, Missouri

"I have often made that wish since an if the buffalo would come back tomorrow I wouldent be slow shedding to a brich clout and youd trade that three duce ranch for a buffalo hoss and a pair ear rings like many I know, your all Injun under the hide and its a sinch you wouldent get home sick in a skin lodge."

Plate 37. *Stolen Horses,* Oil on board, 18″ x 24″, 1898.

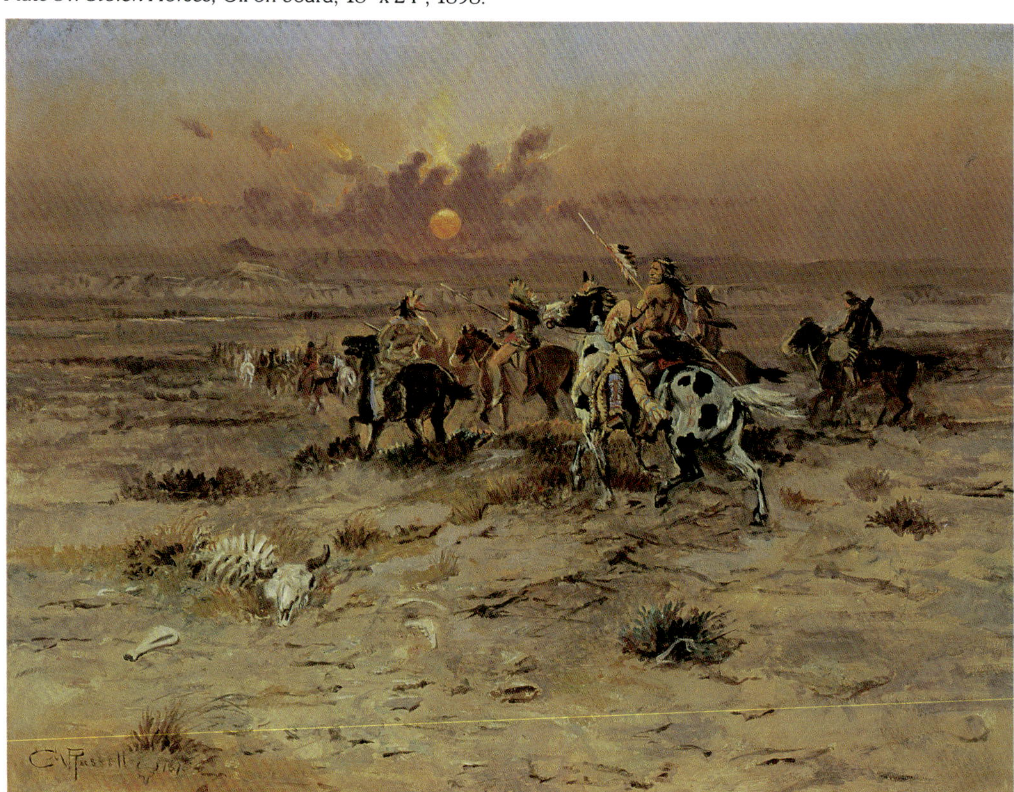

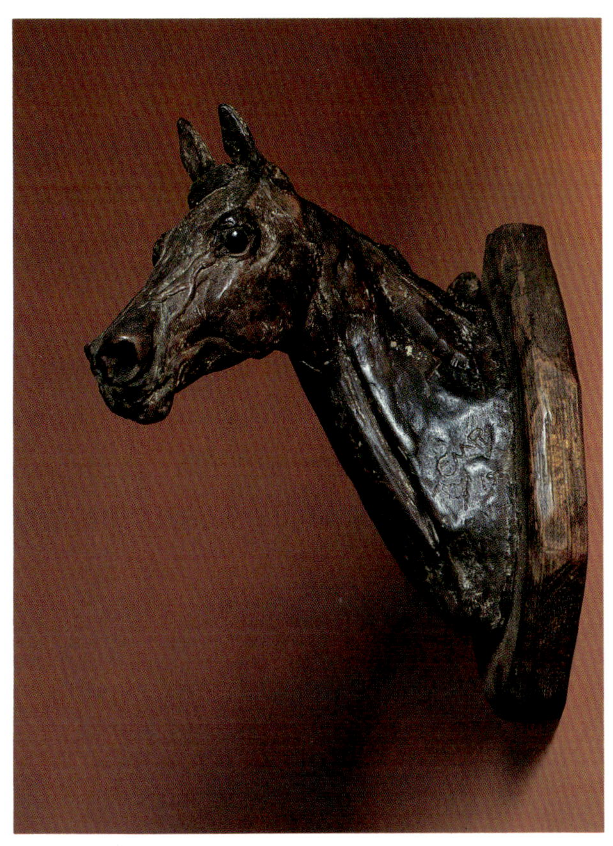

Plate 38. *Bessie B.*,
Beeswax and wood model,
8¼″ x 6½″ x 3½″, 1901.

Plate 39. *Bessie B.*, Bronze,
6⅞″ x 6½″ x 3½″, 1961.

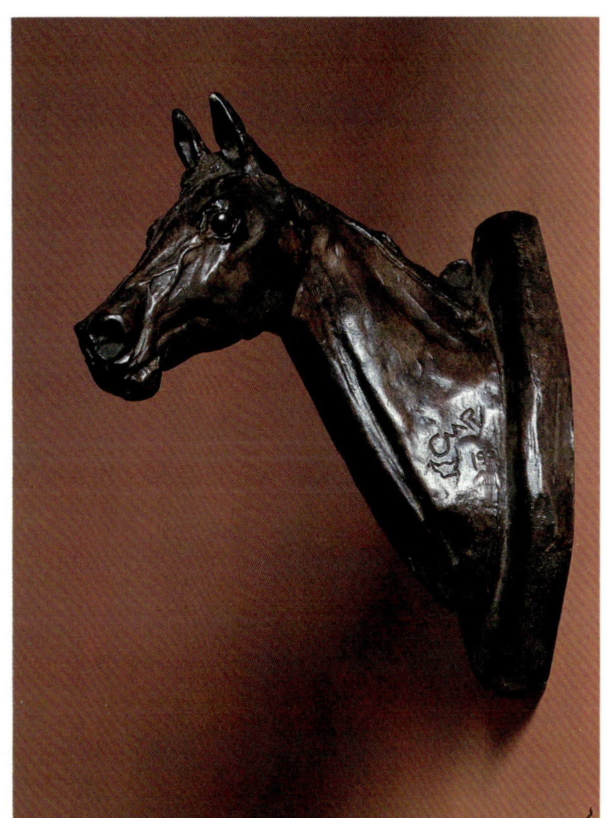

Plate 40. *Sun River War Party,* Oil on canvas, 18″ x 30″, 1903.

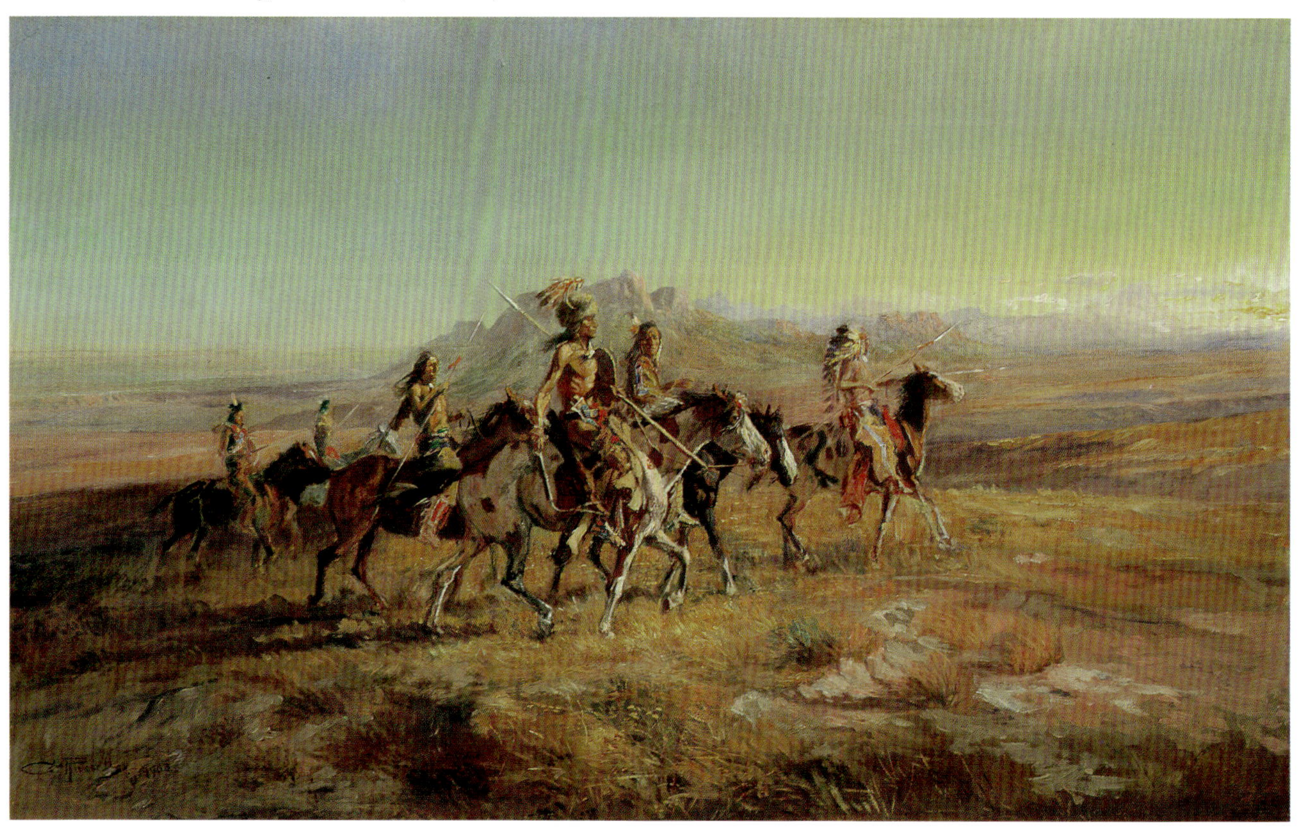

Plate 41. *A Mix Up,* Oil on canvas, 30″ x 48″, 1910.

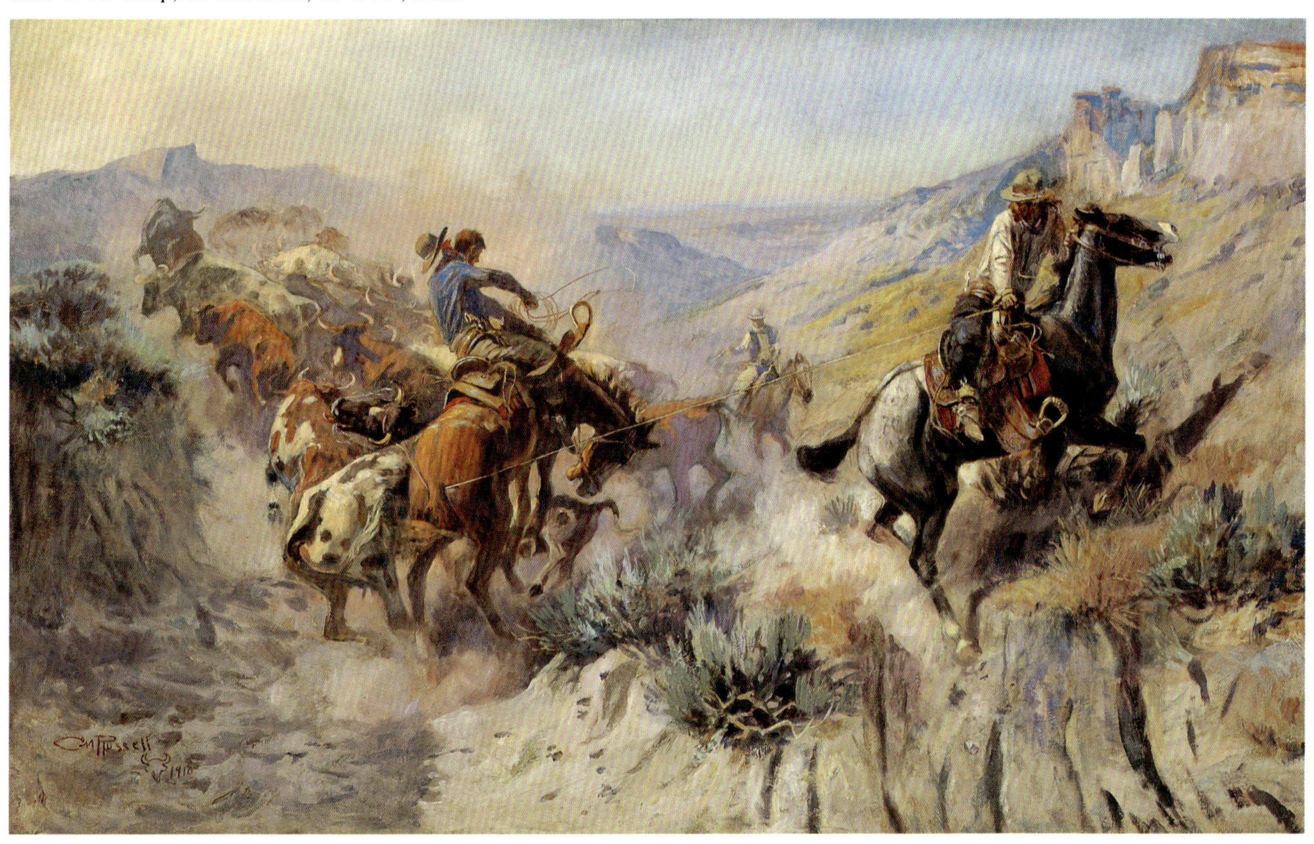

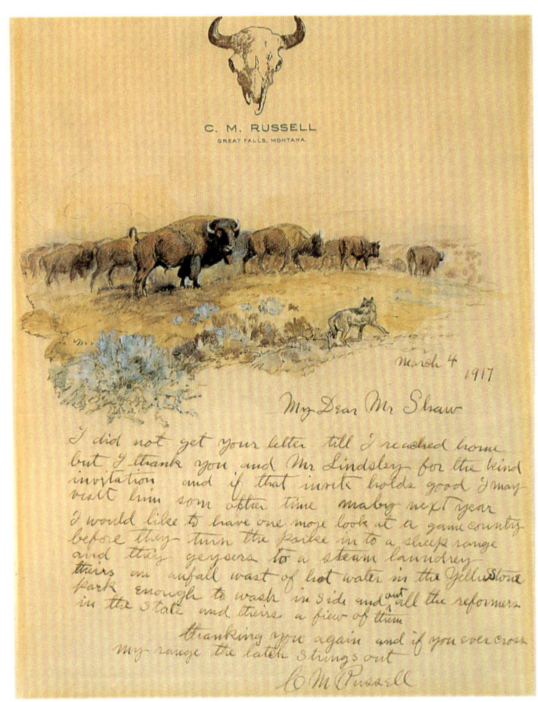
C. M. RUSSELL
GREAT FALLS, MONTANA

March 4
1917

My Dear Mr Shaw

I did not get your letter till I reached home but I thank you and Mr Lindsley for the kind invotation and if that invite holds good I may visit him som other time maby next year I would like to have one more look at a game country before they turn the parke in to a sheep range and they geysers to a steam laundrey theirs an awfull wast of hot water in the Yellowstone park enough to wash in side and out all the reformers in the State and theirs a fiew of them

thanking you again and if you ever cross my range the latch strings out

C M Russell

Plate 42. *A Game Country,*
Illustrated letter,
11″ x 8½″, 1917.

Plate 43. *A Russell Buffalo,*
Bronze, 6⅔″ x 5⅛″ x 4⅔″,
cast in 1961.

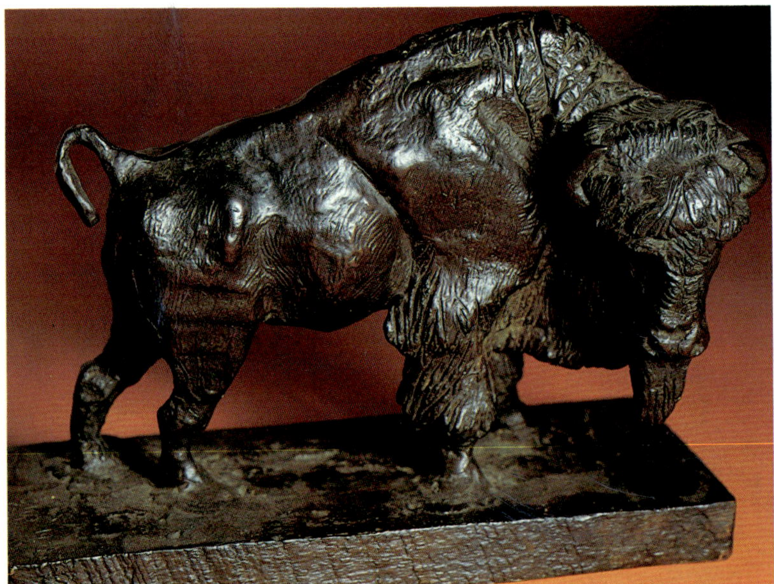

SYDNEY LAURENCE

(1865 – 1940)
b. Brooklyn, New York

"When you get as old as I am you'll know you don't know anything."

Plate 44. *Mt. McKinley,* Oil on canvas, 53″ x 43″, 1922, Gift of Gertrude Brewster.

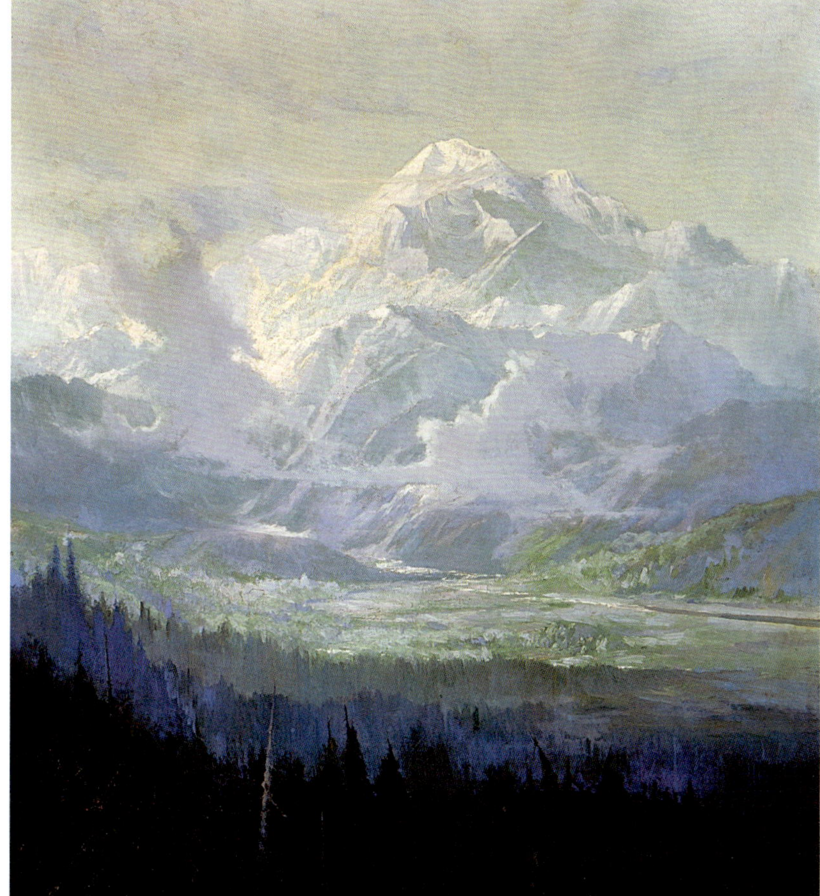

EANGER IRVING COUSE

(1866 – 1936)
b. Saginaw, Michigan

. . . "it is not the fighting Indian Mr. E. Irving Couse depicts. He delights in the Indian of New Mexico, the Pueblo Indian . . . At Taos . . . where Mr. Couse finds his models, thirty miles away from the nearest railroad, he spends his summers painting from the Indian models and from the landscape which so picturesquely sets off the Indian." – anonymous journalist, 1909

Plate 45. *The Apprentice,* Oil on canvas, 35″ x 46″, n.d.

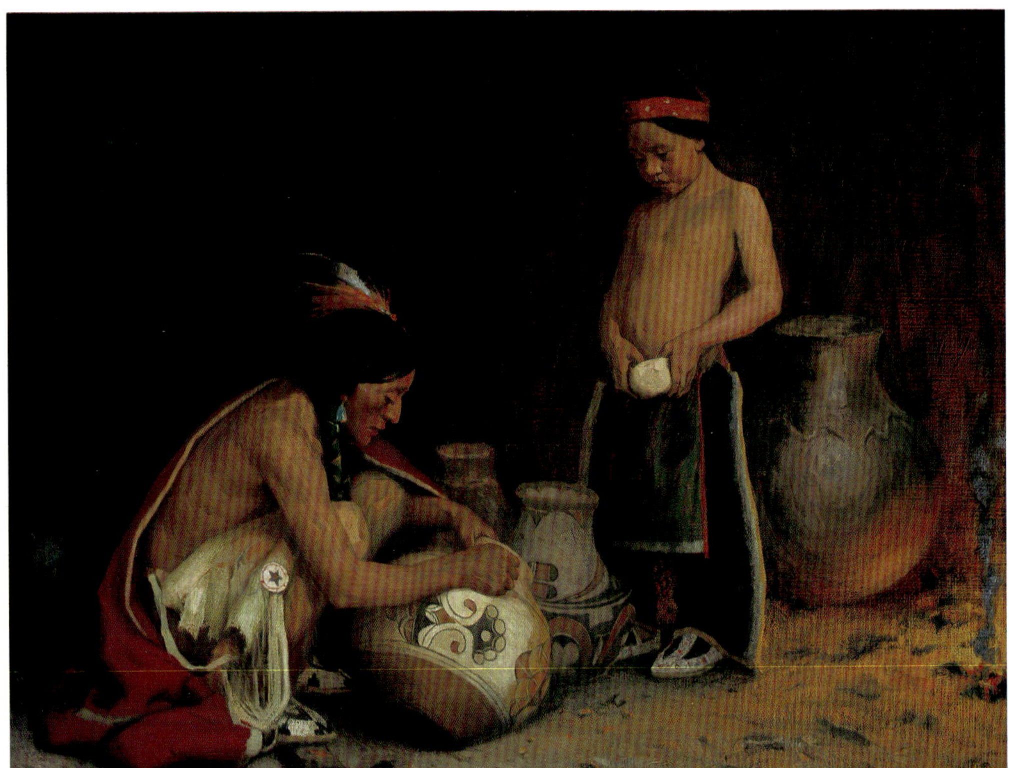

Plate 46. *The Early Picture Makers,* or *Montezuma's Legend,* Oil on canvas, 7¾" x 9¾", 1925.

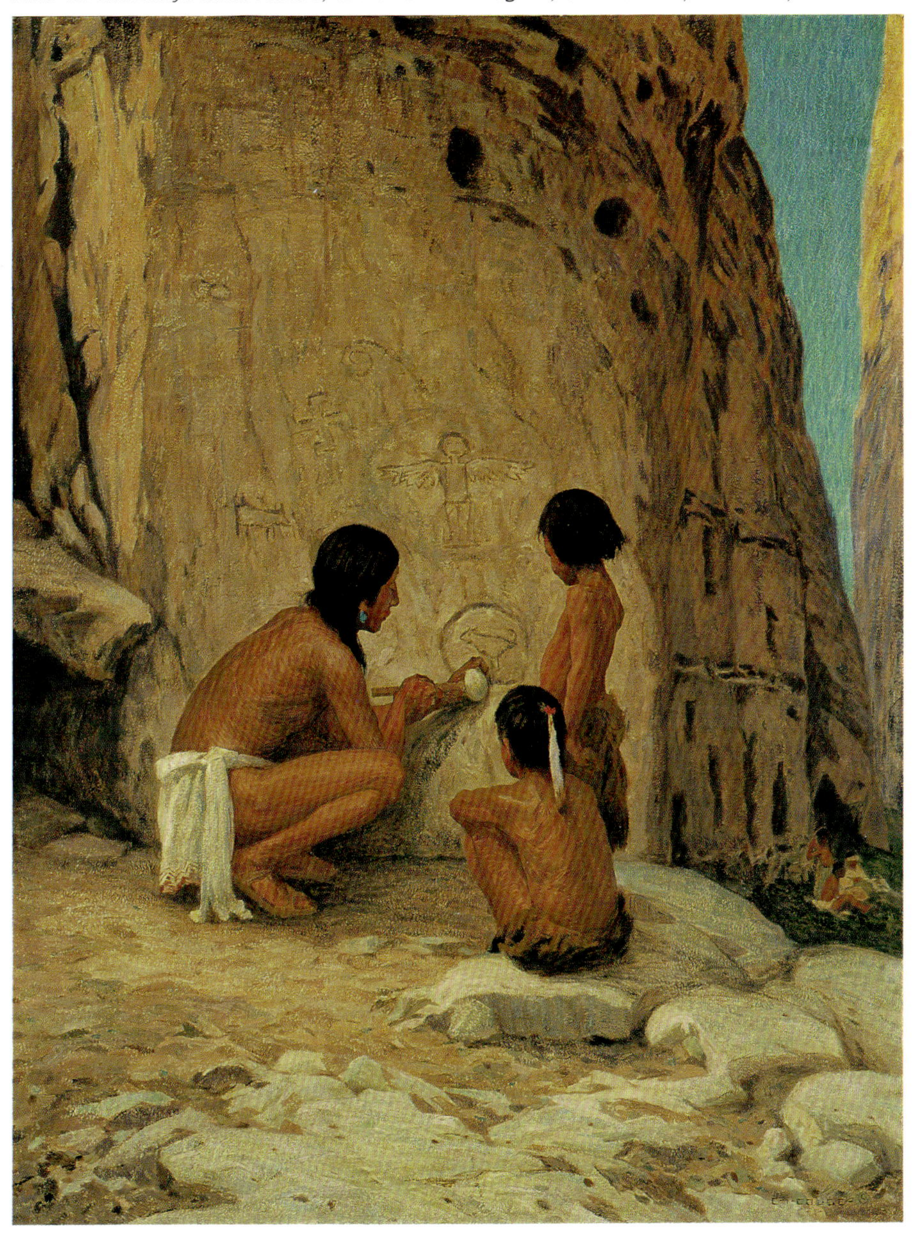

WILLIAM ROBINSON LEIGH

(1866 – 1955)
b. Berkeley County, West Virginia

. . . "I had been electrified. I saw with brand new eyes my drawing lacked the subtlety of action of the original. Action! A whole new world opened up before me. Action was all-important. Without it nothing was any good. I saw now why my drawing did not satisfy. I saw what must be done to make it live. Sing." – 1952

Plate 47. *Return of the War Canoes,*
Oil on canvas, 27¼" x 21½", 1920.

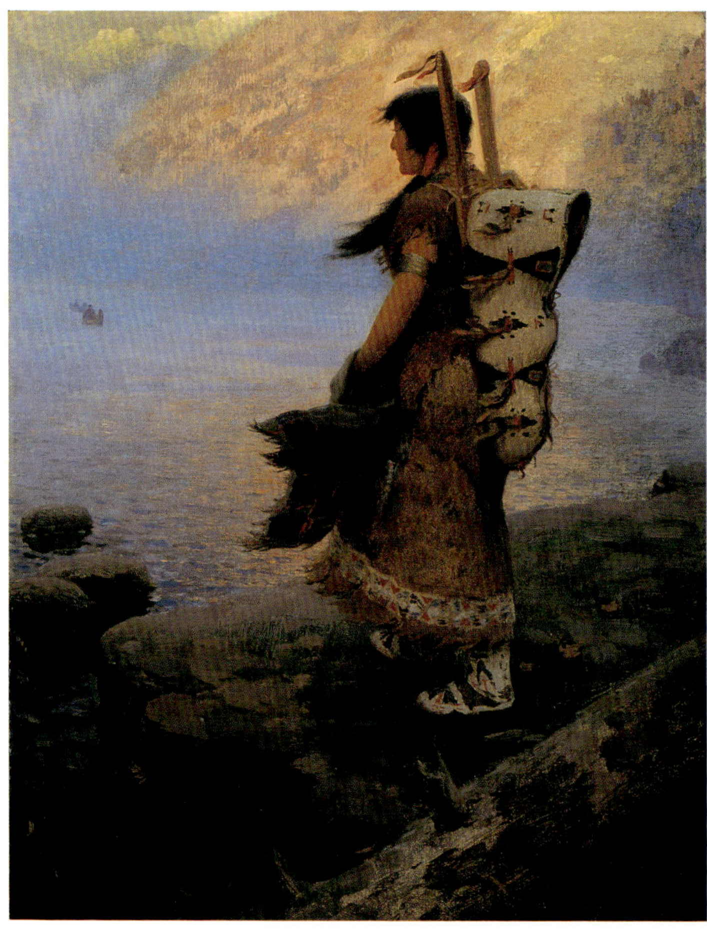

Plate 48. *The Great Buffalo Hunt,* Oil on canvas, 78⅛″ x 126¼″, 1947.

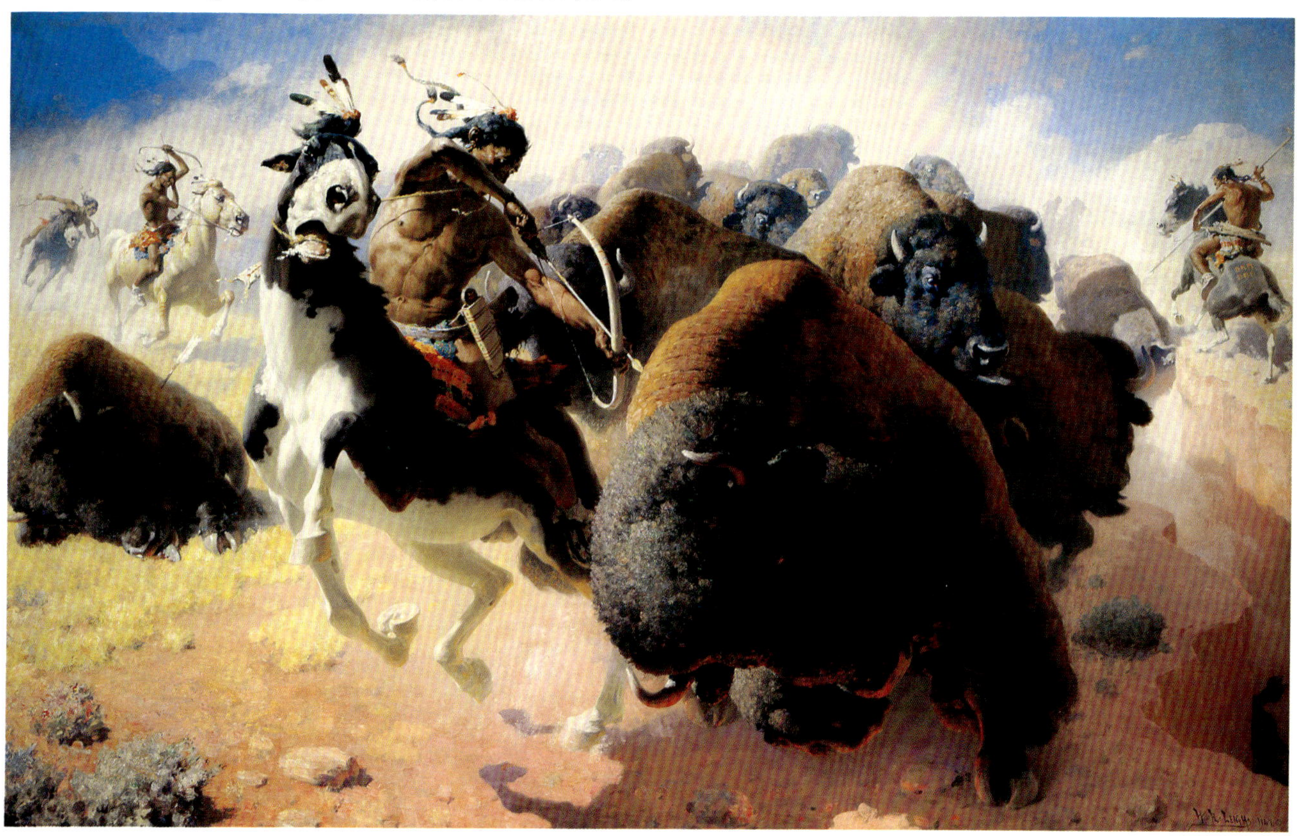

CARL RUNGIUS

(1869 – 1959)
b. Berlin, Germany

"[In the Rockies] I felt strongly the urge to paint straight landscape – that is, landscape for its own sake. Until then I had considered landscape only as a setting for big game animals. But the grandeur of the mountains with the marvelous atmospheric conditions in Alberta and consequent color effects changed all of that."

Plate 49. *The Monarchs of the Wilderness,* Oil on canvas, 36″ x 56″, ca. 1901.

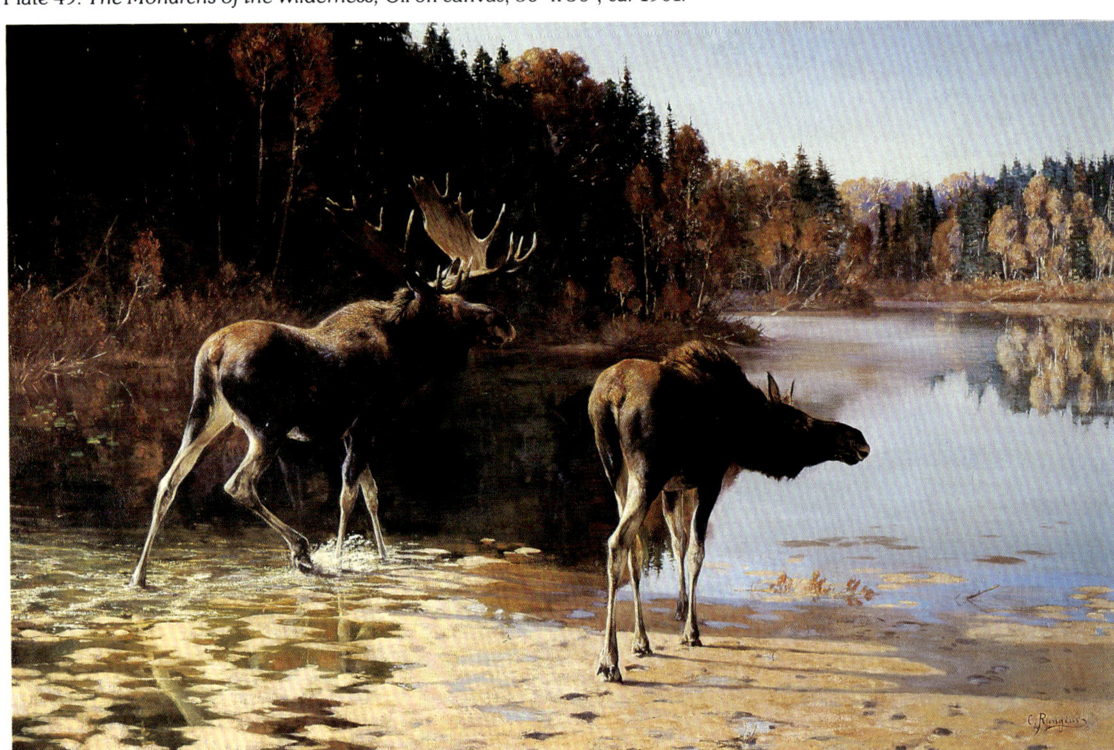

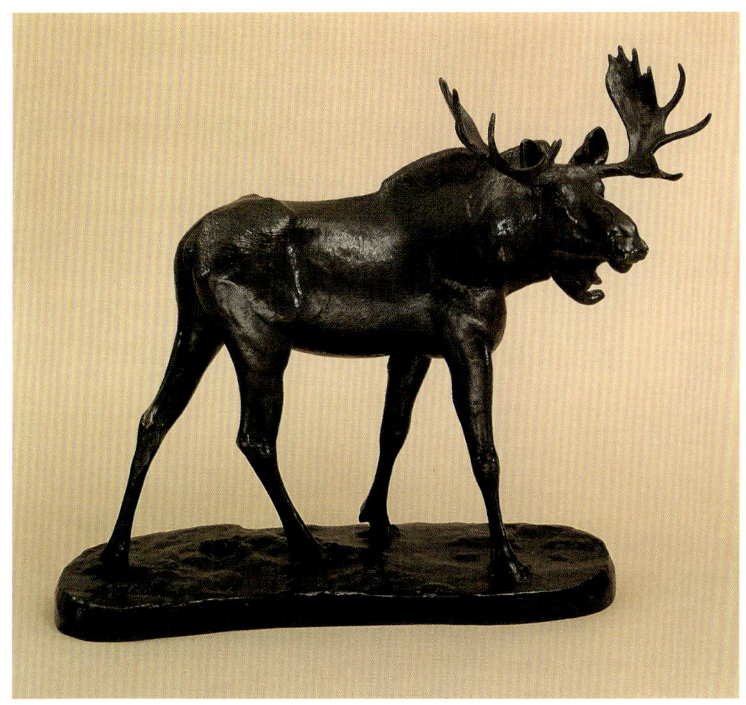

Plate 50. *Bull Moose,* Bronze,
17″ x 17″ x 8″, 1905,
Collection of Robert F. Rockwell, Jr.

Plate 51. *Bighorn Sheep,* Bronze,
17¾″ x 16½″ x 6½″, 1915,
Collection of Robert F. Rockwell, Jr.

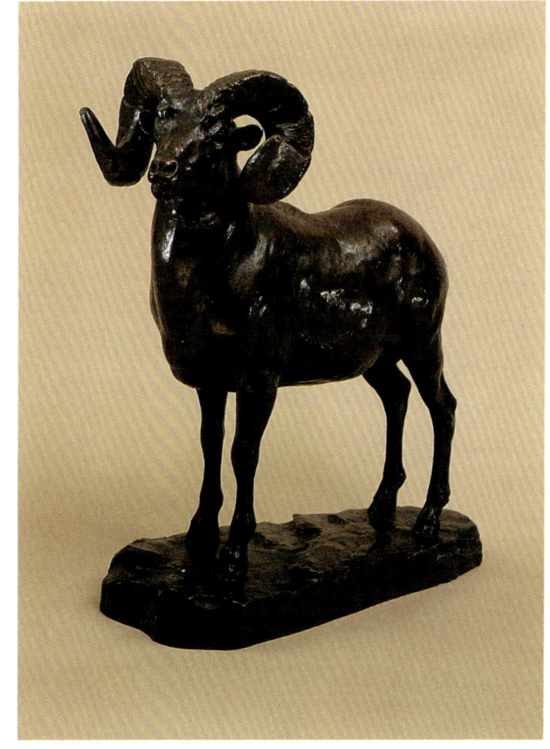

Plate 52. *In the Bighorn Country*, Oil on canvas, 28" x 90", ca. 1943.

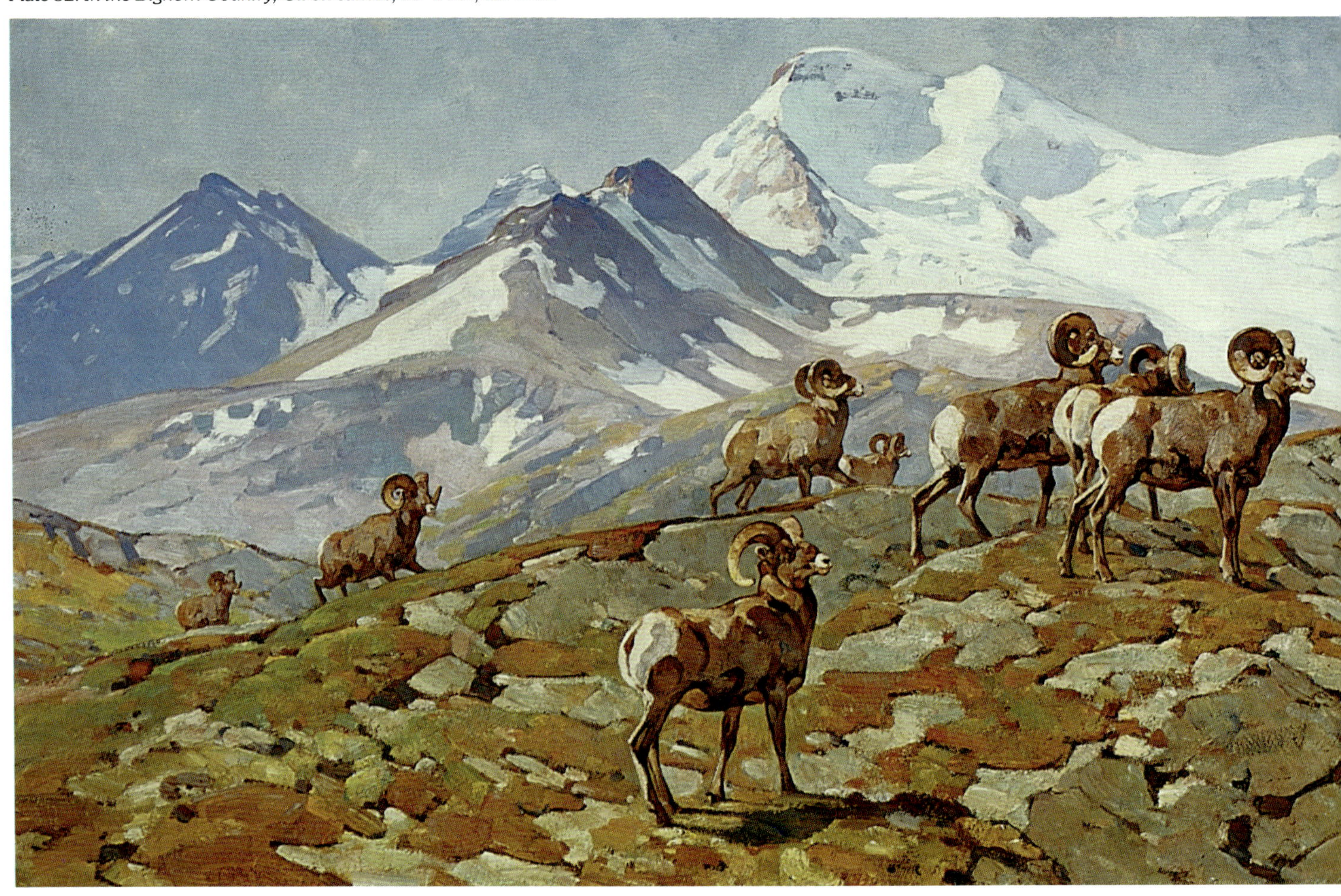

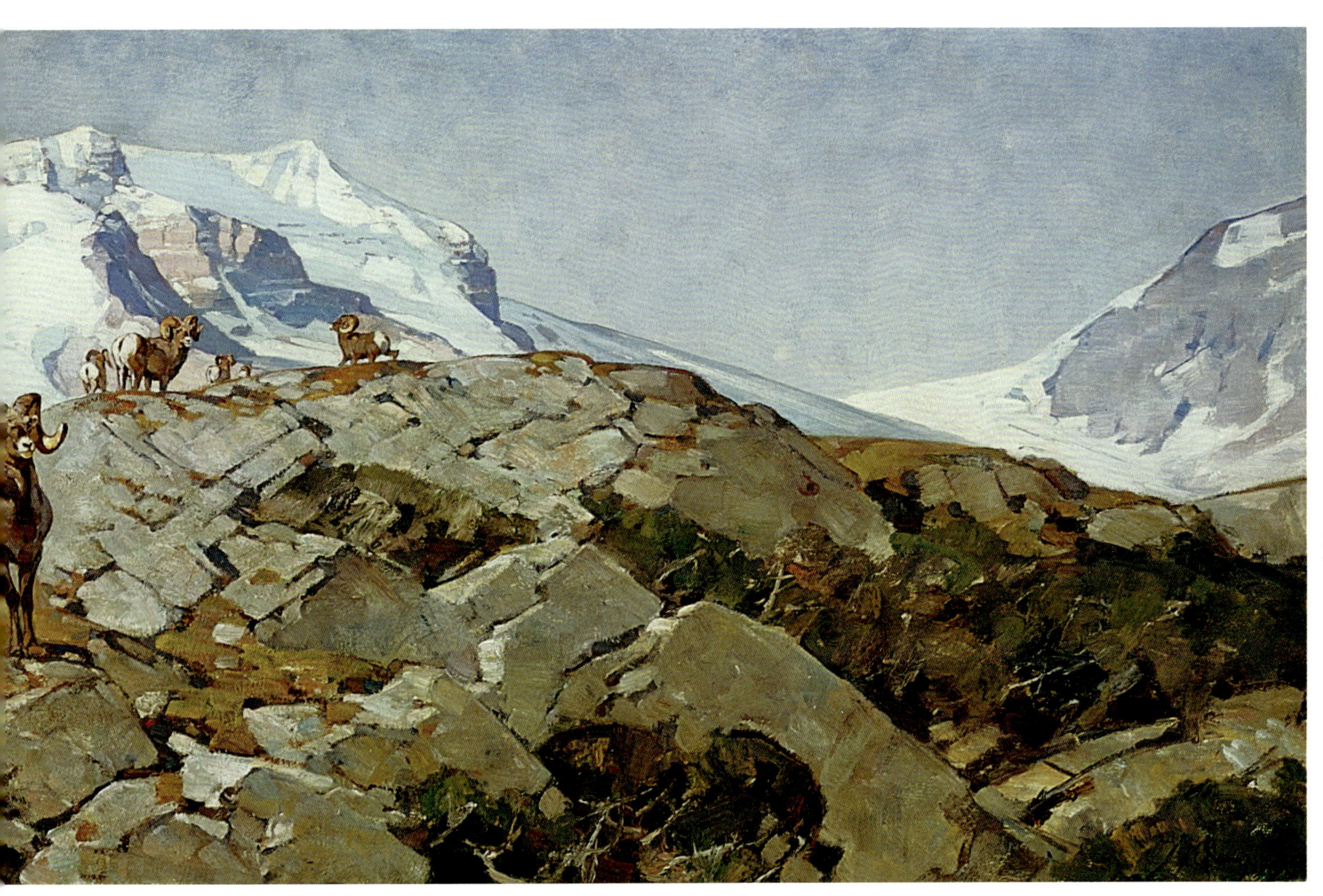

HENRY MERWIN SHRADY

(1871 – 1922)
b. New York, New York

Plate 53. *Elk Buffalo,* Bronze, 23″ x 32″ x 12″, 1900.

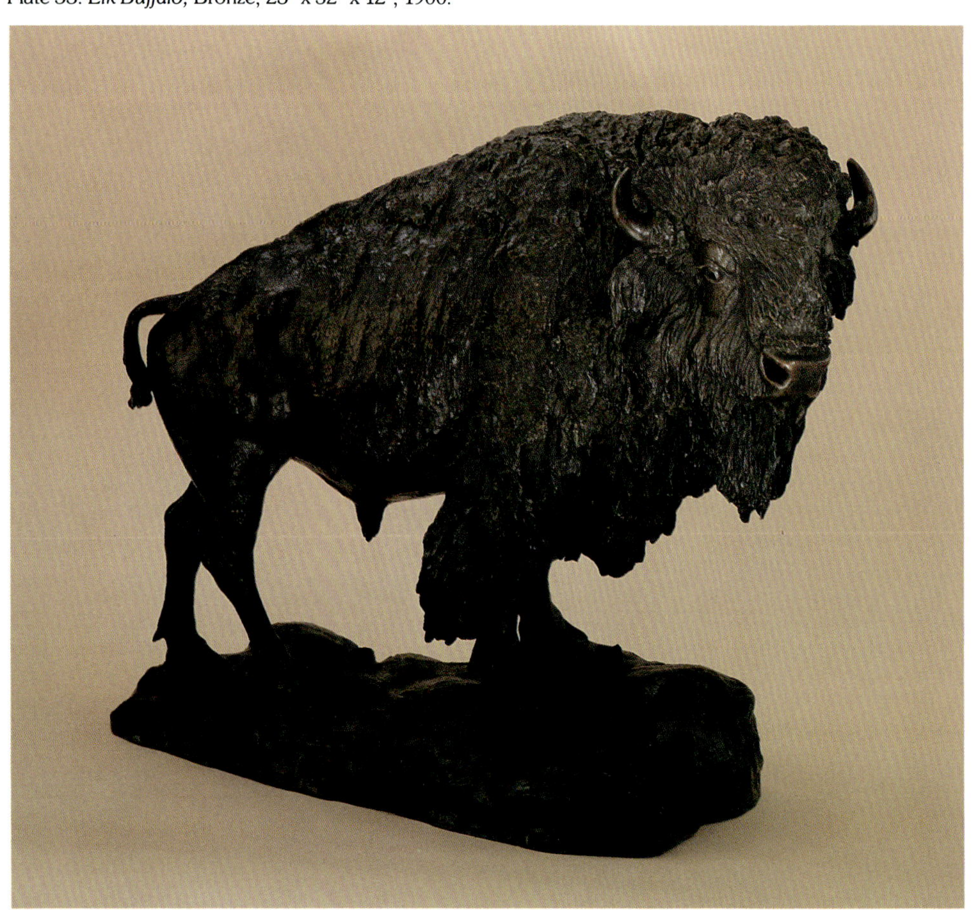

(JOHN) EDWARD BOREIN

(1872 – 1945)
b. San Leandro, California

"I will leave only an accurate history of the West, nothing else but that. If anything isn't authentic or just right, I won't put it in any of my work."

Plate 54. *The Calgary Stampede,* Gouache, 14¾" x 36¼", sight, 1916.

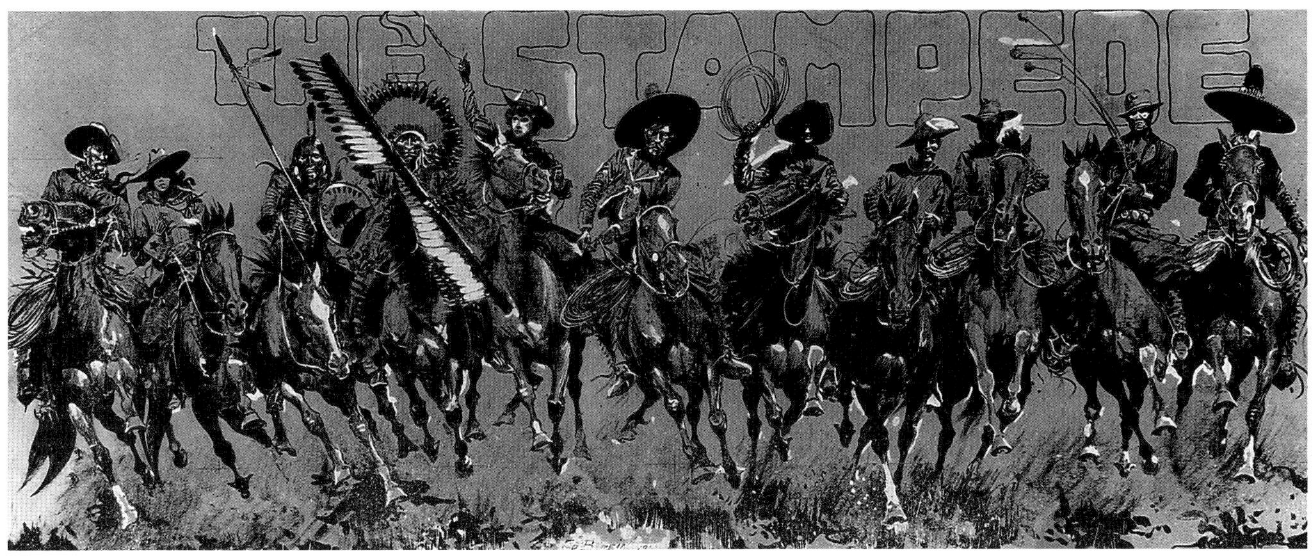

Plate 55. *Three Buckaroos,* Watercolor, 11″ x 15⅝″, ca. 1920, Collection of Hertha Rockwell.

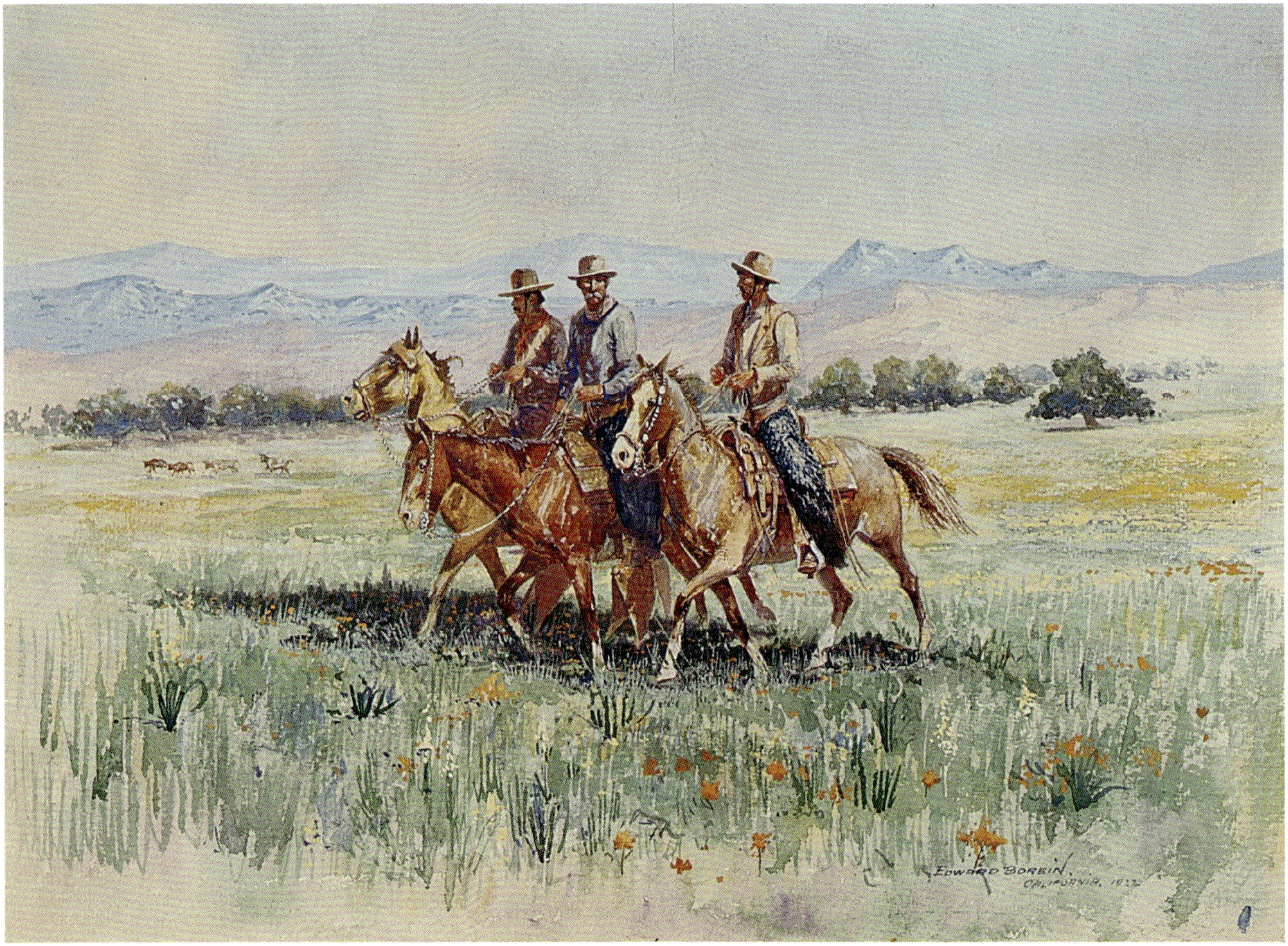

FRANK TENNEY JOHNSON

(1874 – 1939)
b. Big Grove, Iowa

"This makes one week that I have been right amongst the Navajos every day – seeing new ones all the time – watching them at their games, racing and selling horses, visiting trading posts and dancing in the moonlight. It has been a wonderful thing for me – which I shall never forget." – 1904

Plate 56. *The Morning Shower,* Oil on canvas, 36″ x 28″, 1927.

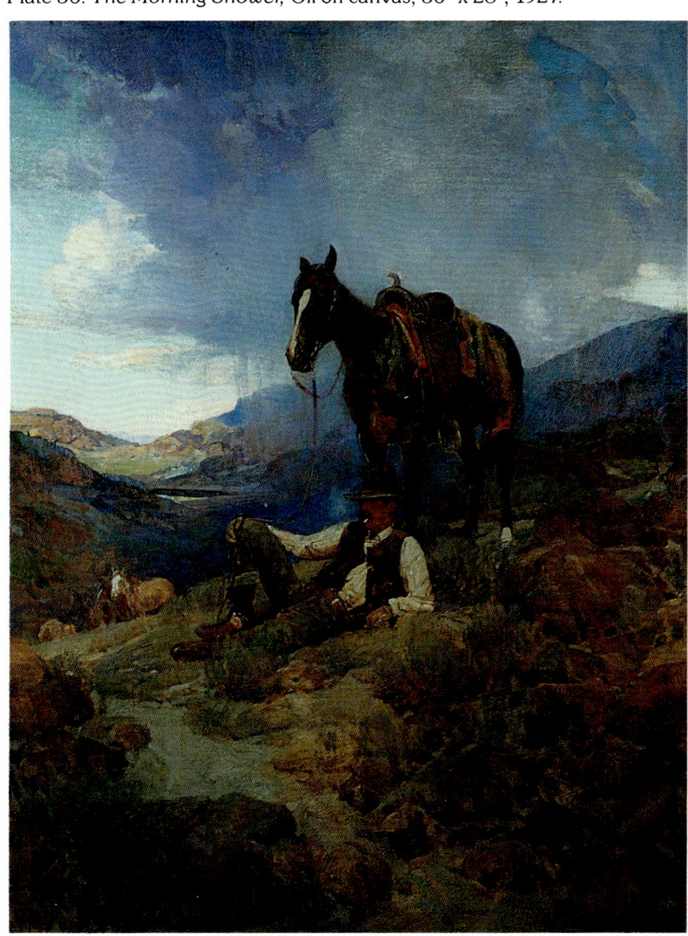

OSCAR EDMUND BERNINGHAUS

(1874 – 1952)
b. St. Louis, Missouri

"I think the colony in Taos is doing much for American art. From it I think will come a distinctive art, something definitely American – and I do not mean that such will be the case because the American Indian and his environment are the subjects. But the canvases that come from Taos are as definitely American as anything can be. We have had French, Dutch, Italian, German art. Now we must have American art. I feel that from Taos will come that art."

Plate 57. *Indians,* Oil on canvas, 35¼" x 29¼", sight, 1920, Collection of Robert F. Rockwell, Jr.

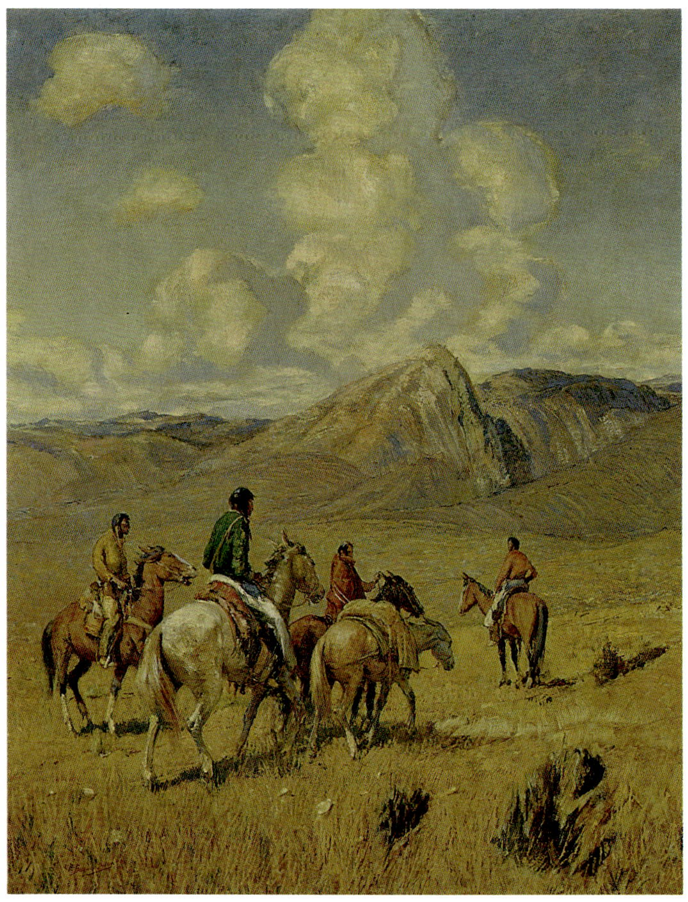

WALTER UFER
(1876 – 1936)
b. Louisville, Kentucky

"I paint the Indian as he is. In the garden digging – in the field working – riding amongst the sage – meeting his woman in the desert – angling for trout – in meditation."

Plate 58. *Along the Rio Grande,* or *New Mexican Pastime,* Oil on canvas, 24½″ x 24½, 1920.

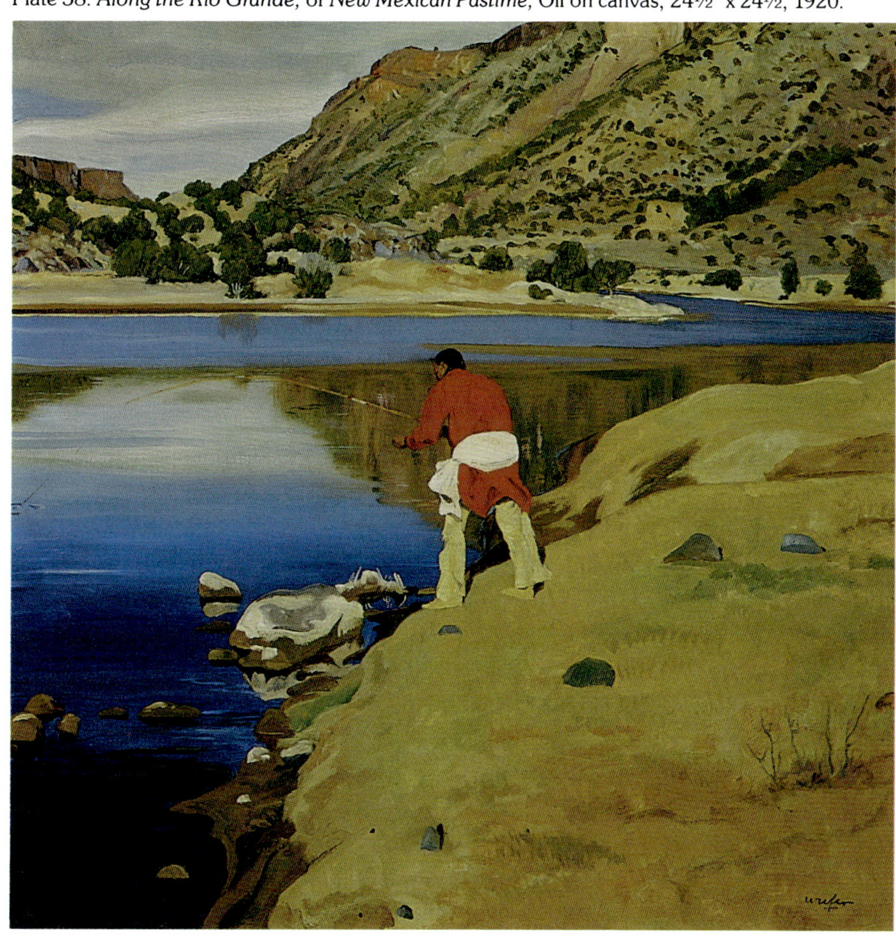

JAMES EARLE FRASER

(1876–1953)
b. Winona, Minnesota

"A long time ago, when I was a small boy . . . I lived in the Indian country of Dakota, in the land that belonged to the Indians, and I saw them in their villages, crossing the prairies on their hunting expeditions. Often they stopped beside our ranch house; and camped and traded rabbits and other game for chickens. They seemed very happy until the order came to place them on reservations. One group after another was surrounded by soldiers and herded beyond the Missouri River. I realised that they were always being sent farther West, and I often heard my father say that the Indians would some day be pushed into the Pacific Ocean, and I think that accounted for my sympathetic feeling for them."

Plate 59. *End of the Trail*, Bronze, 44½" x 33½" x 13", 1908.

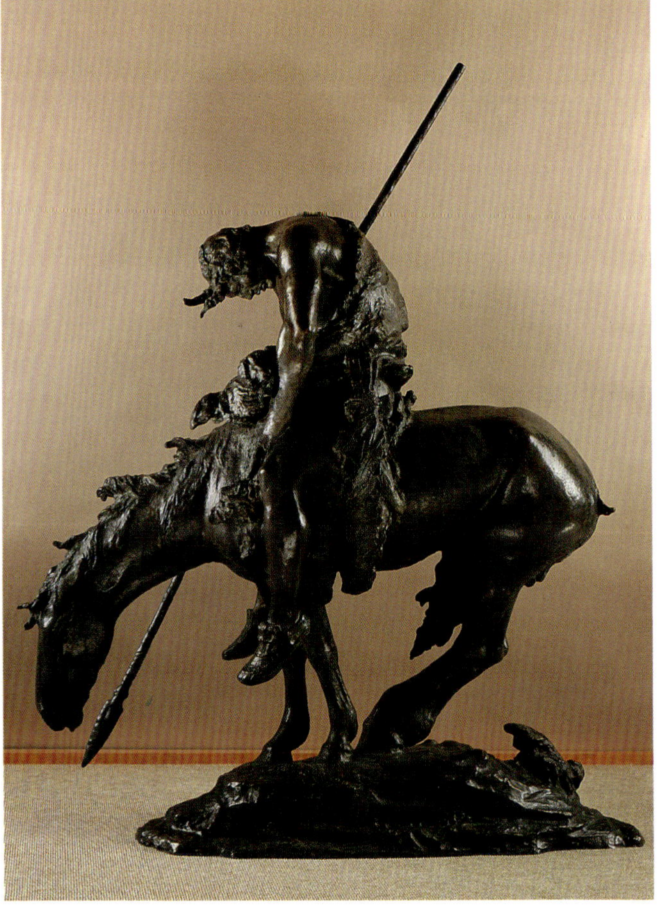

OLAF CARL BØRRE SELTZER

(1877 – 1957)
b. Copenhagen, Denmark

"If there is anything of lasting value in my art, it will survive. If not, it will perish."

Plate 60. *Fool's Fire,* Oil on canvas, 24″ x 36″, 1920.

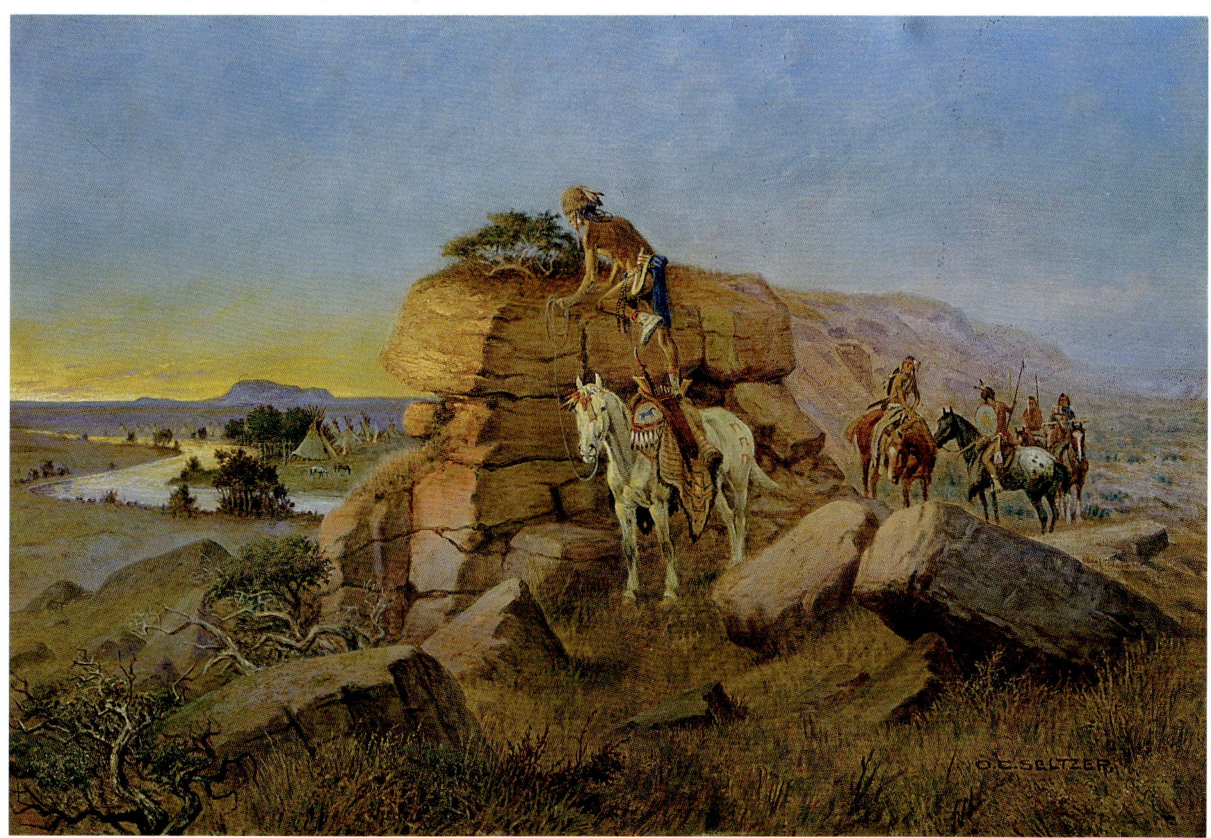

WILLIAM HERBERT DUNTON

(1878 – 1936)
b. Augusta, Maine

"The West has passed – more's the pity. In another 25 years the old-time westerners will have gone, too – gone with the buffalo and the antelope. I'm going to hand down to posterity a bit of the unadulterated real thing." – *1925*

Plate 61. *The Helping Hand,* Oil on canvas, 24½" x 37½", sight, 1910, Collection of Robert F. Rockwell, Jr.

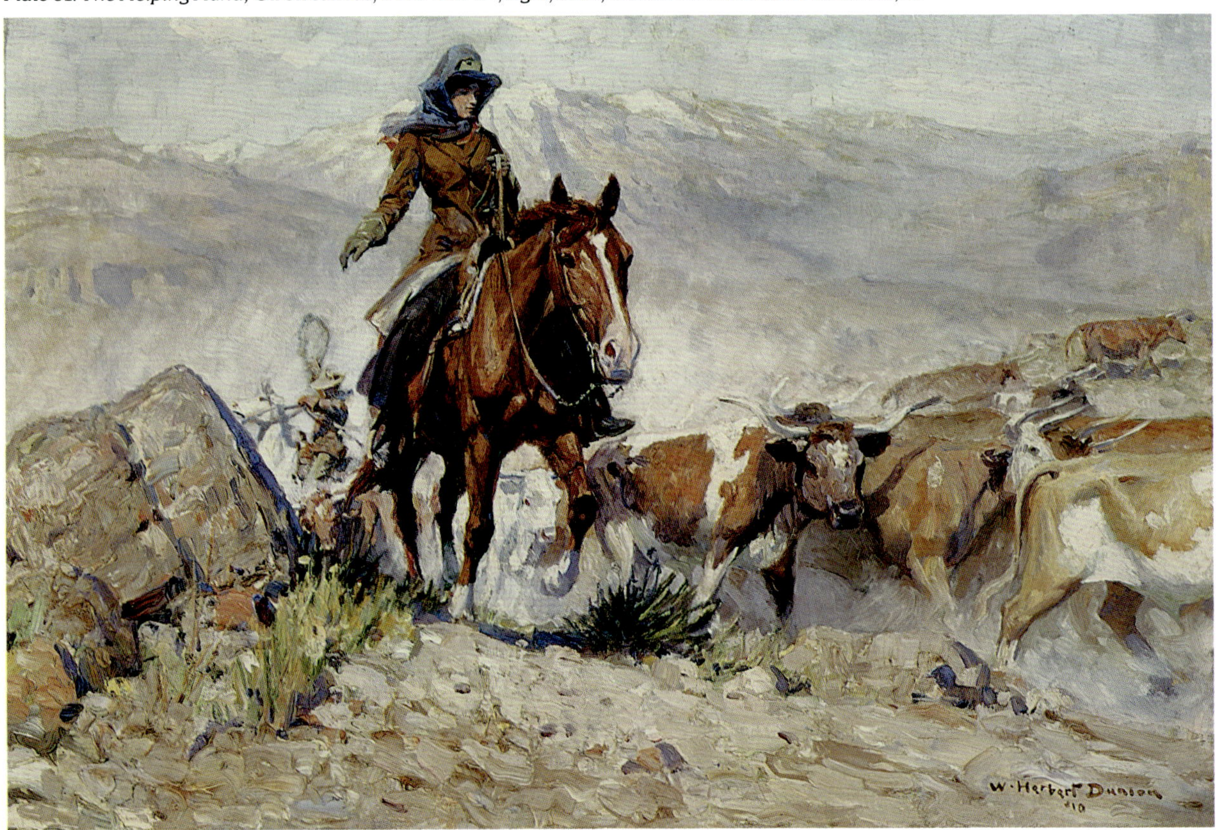

WILLIAM HENRY DETHLEF KOERNER

(1878 – 1938)
b. Lun, Germany

"You have to see the life *of the tree and only a great man can see life, ever-present life. Another thing you must grasp is that a tree has roots. An artist must realize that it must go into the ground with a root system as strong and as wide-spreading as its branches.* Think of roots *when you paint a tree and then your painting of a tree will not be on top of the earth; it will* go into *the earth."*

Plate 62. *Alcalde's Welcome to Taos,* Oil on canvas, 27" x 39", ca. 1931.

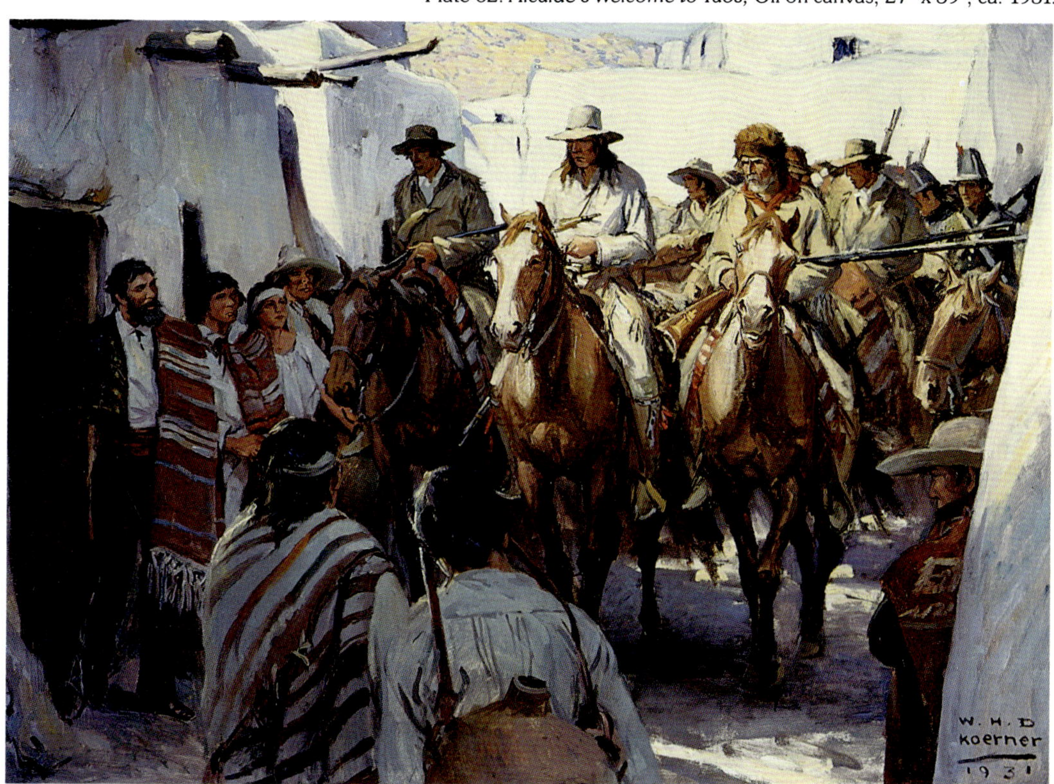

HARVEY T. DUNN
(1884 – 1952)
b. Manchester, South Dakota

"Before one can be an illustrator, one must be an artist . . . If a picture is good, you can tell nothing of the artist in a personal way. If a picture is bad, you can tell all about the painter. A man may lie to me and I will believe him. But let the same man paint a picture, and he cannot lie successfully – his fault is most plain."

Plate 63. *Montana Winter Scene,*
Oil on canvas, 36¼" x 24", sight, 1907,
Gift of James McMahon.

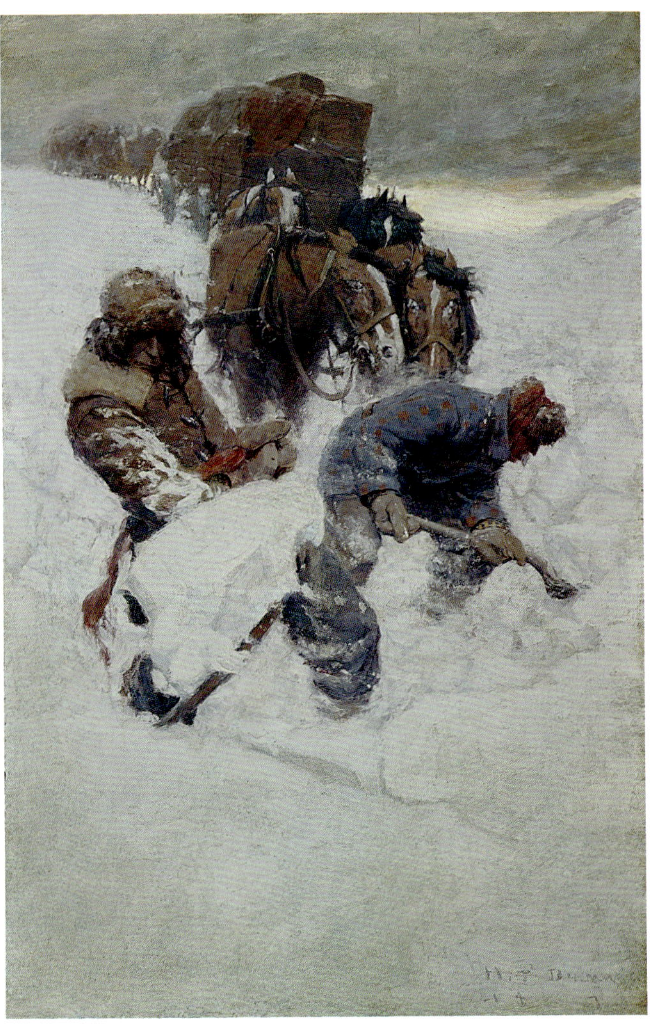

ERNEST MARTIN HENNINGS

(1886 – 1956)
b. Pennsgrove, New Jersey

"A painting is a great adventure – thinking over a subject, making all sorts of pencil sketches, designing, comparing, organizing, planning its color, the lighting, until you are sure it has everything that you want [in order to be] strong and effective. Then you go to work on your canvas, with your models, and this will call for all the ability and craftsmanship which the years of work have given you, plus all the special effort you are capable of in order to have a consummative and significant piece of art realized."

Plate 64. *The Teacher* or *Songs of Old,* Oil on canvas, 15½" x 19¼", sight, ca. 1925.

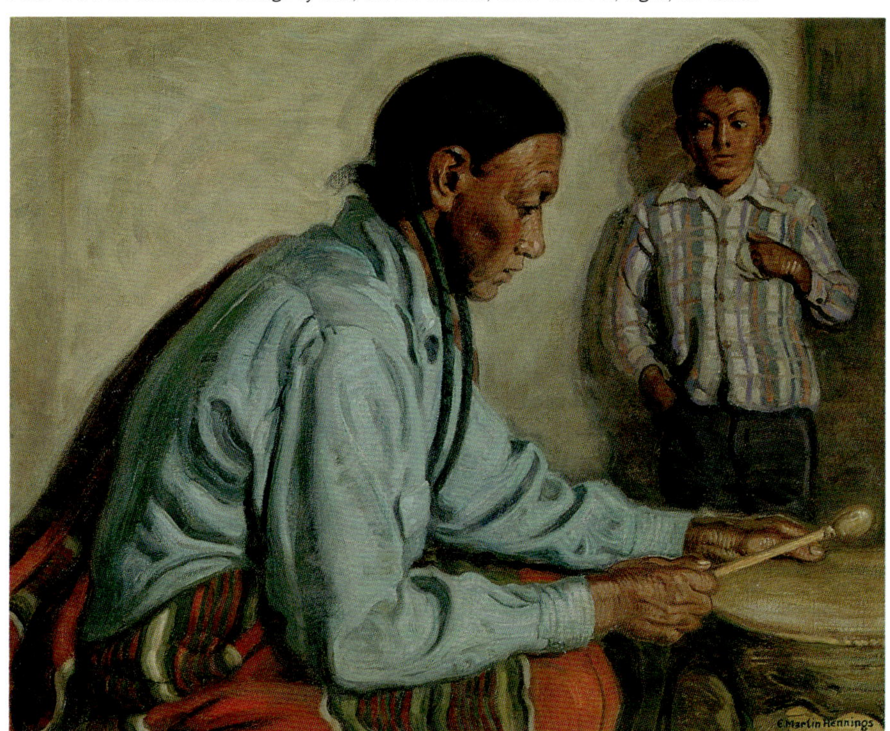

RAPHAEL LILLYWHITE

(1891 – 1958)
b. Woodruff, Arizona

"The highest form of creative work which man can do is to indulge in the forming of his own character and personality."

Plate 65. *Teed and Bluedog,* Oil on canvas, 24¾" x 30", sight, ca. 1940, Collection of Robert F. Rockwell, Jr.

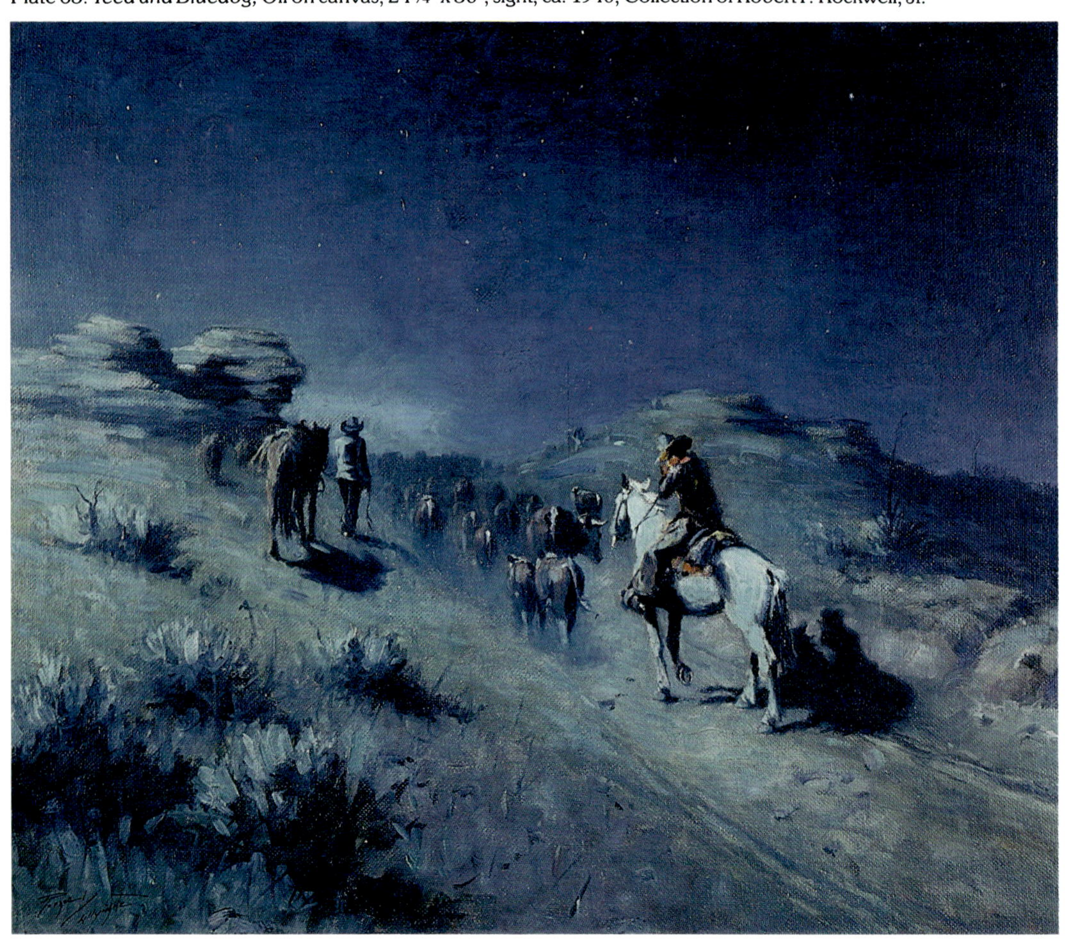

HAROLD VON SCHMIDT

(1893–1982)
b. Alameda, California

"As painters, we must remember always that the spirit is more important than the fact."

Plate 66. *Rustlers at Work,* Oil on paperboard, 30″ x 50″, 1934.

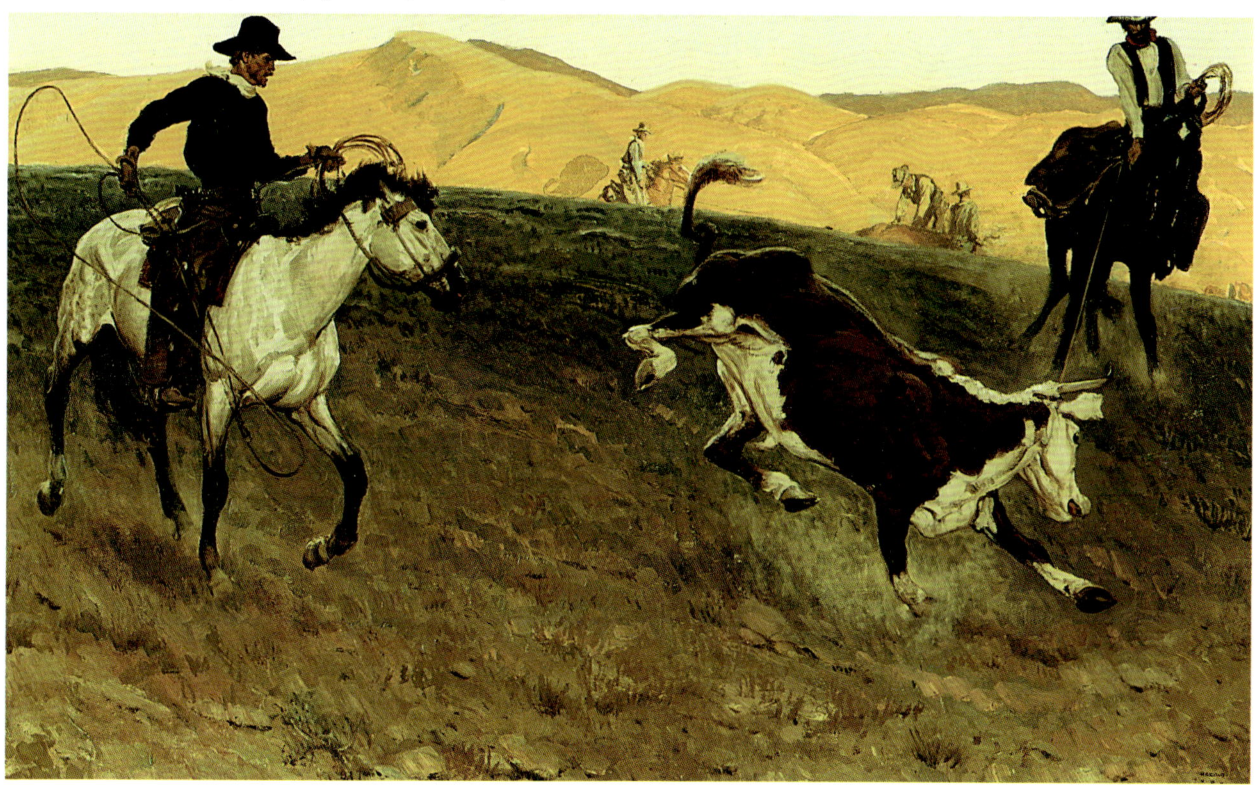

NICK EGGENHOFER

(1897 – 1985)
b. Gauting, Germany

"Since the horse was of such tremendous importance in the development of the west, the young artist should at least get on a horse and ride once in a while. This does not mean he has to become a champion rider or expert roper, but it is vitally important to know what it feels like to sit a horse. If not, it will show up in your art very quickly."

Plate 67. *The Buffalo Hunt*, Oil on canvas, 27½" x 39½", sight, 1960, Collection of Robert F. Rockwell, Jr.

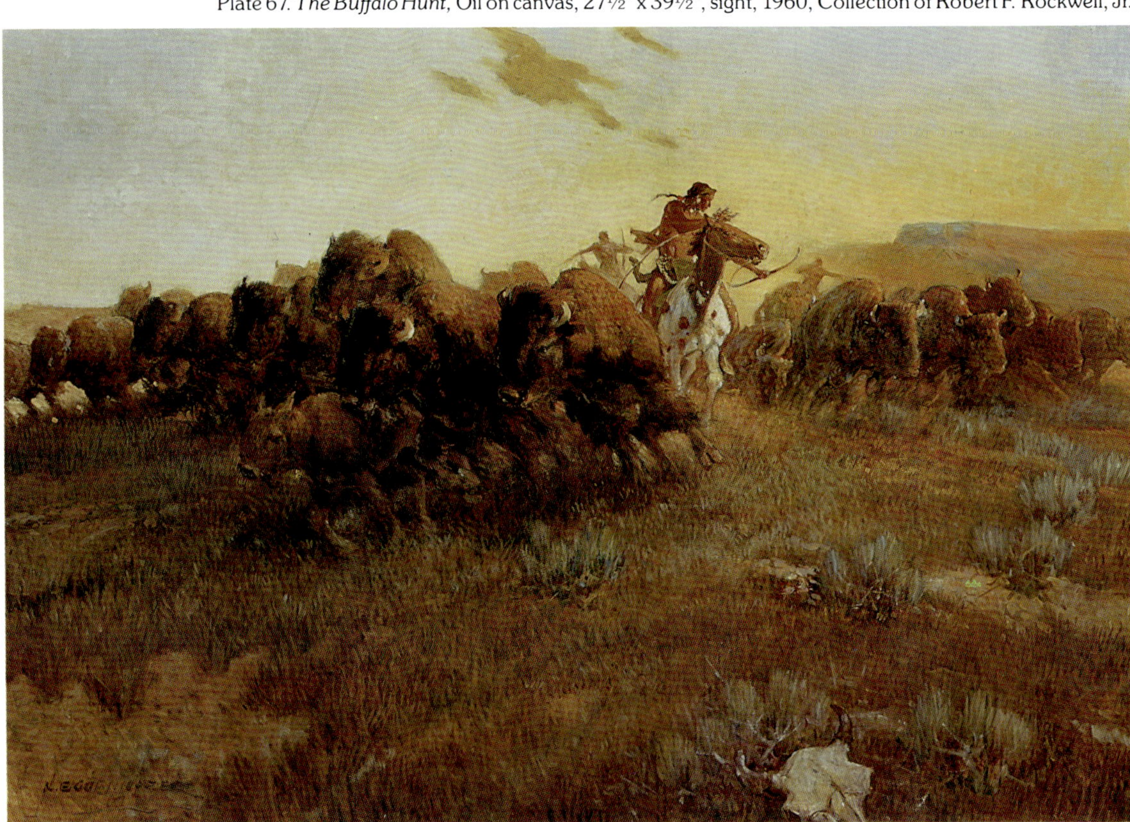

OGDEN MINTON PLEISSNER

(1905 – 1983)
b. Brooklyn, New York

"I find that I can learn more about what I am doing by going outside somewhere, in nature, and walking through the fields or climbing the mountains or walking down a street and looking at the thing as such rather than going through the hands of another artist. I love to look, and get the biggest kick from a good Constable, Homer, Turner, or Monet, and so forth; but I really don't learn a great deal from a picture."

Plate 68. *Lost Lake,* Oil on canvas, 24″ x 30″, 1940.

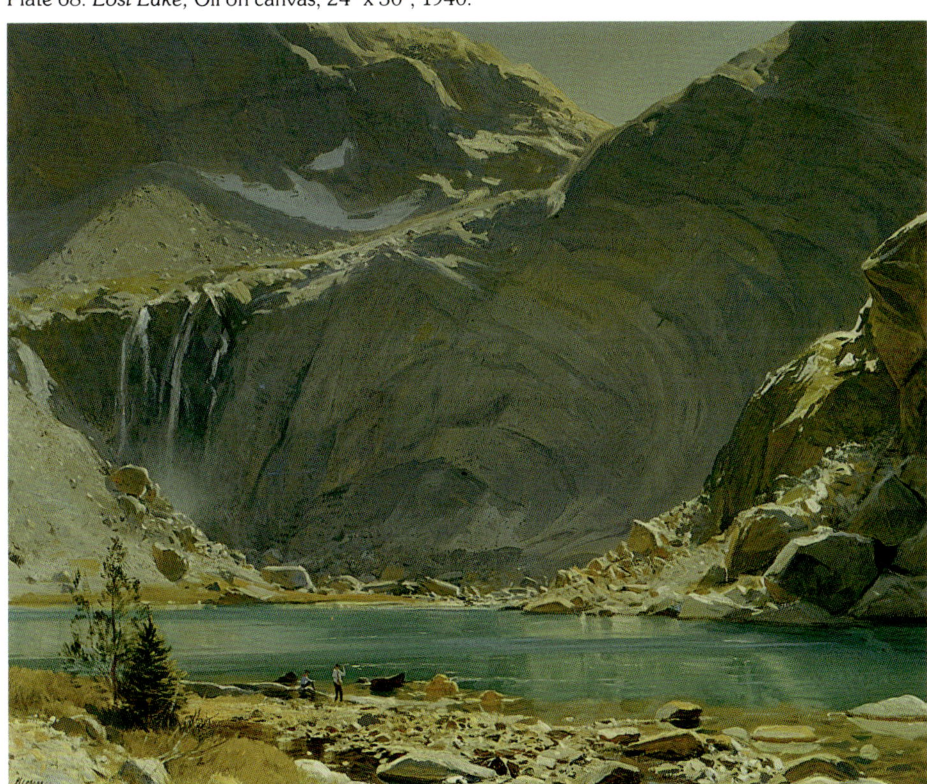

CHARLES "CHARLIE" R. C. DYE

(1906 – 1973)
b. Canon City, Colorado

"I think [people] who have a sincere romance going with the West can sense when an artist is just painting from the fingertips out and not with his heart. Charlie was one artist who used his fingertips and a brush to say what his heart felt about the West." –Joe Beeler

Plate 69. *Come and Get It,* Oil on canvas, 29⅝" x 39½", sight, 1961, Bequest of Clara S. Peck.

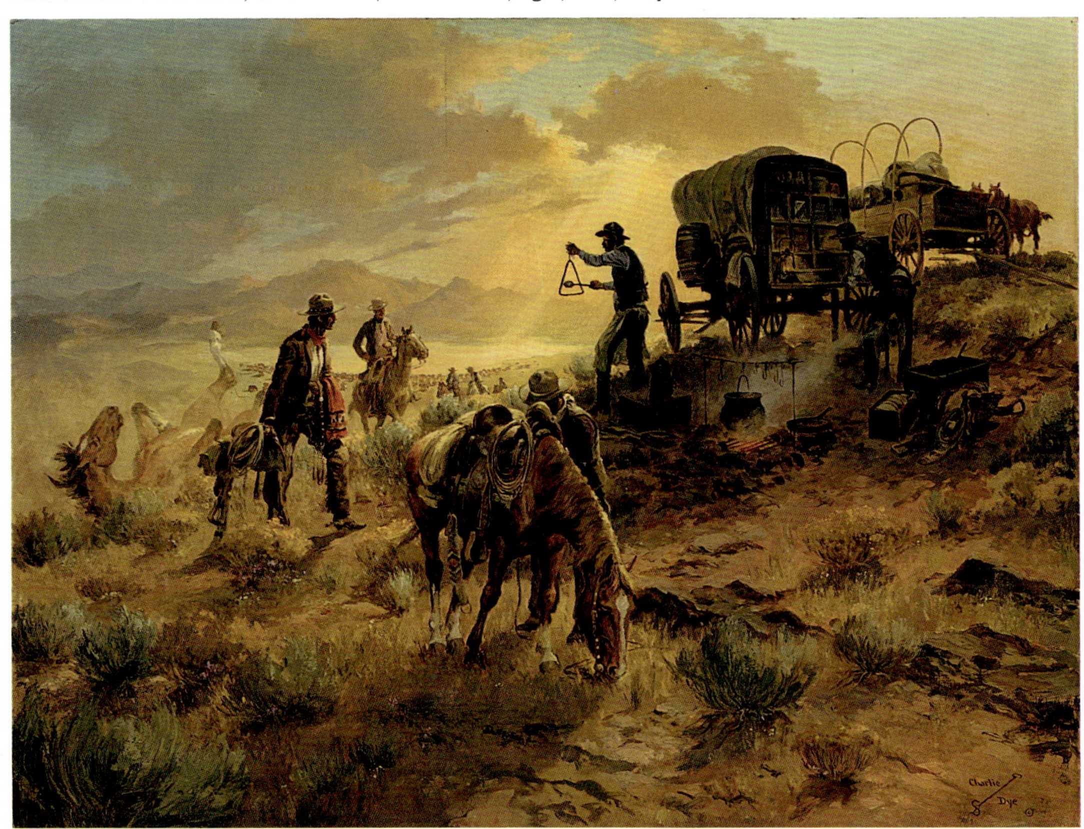

JOHN FORD CLYMER

(1907–   )
b. Ellensburg, Washington

"All painting is just learning to be observant. The more one learns, the more one is able to recognize how things happen with shapes, light and color."

Plate 70. *Time of Hunger,* Oil on canvas, 26" x 42", sight, 1975.

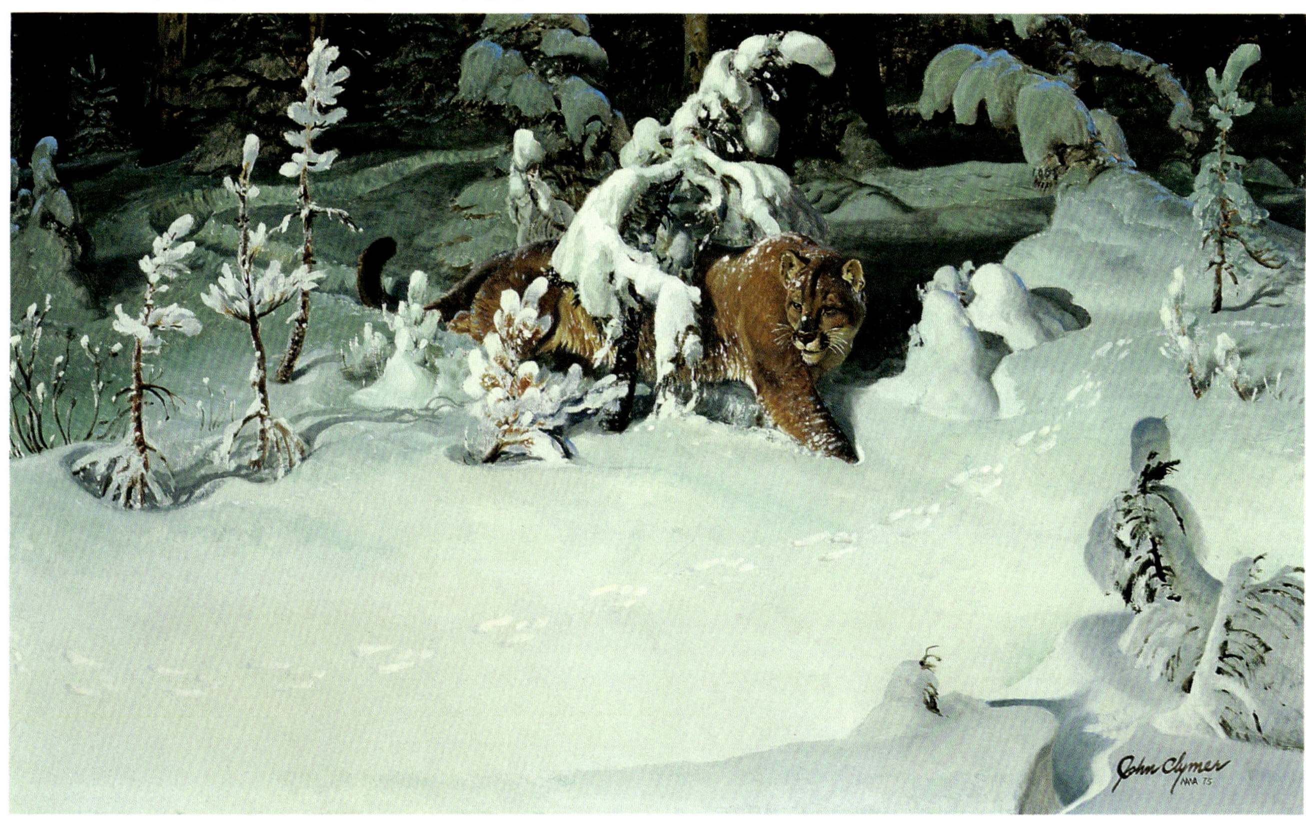

EARLE ERIK HEIKKA
(1910 – 1941)
b. Belt, Montana

Comments on a sculpture entitled "Quartz Team":
"There turned out to be a lot more work on it than I had first expected, and hope that amount of detail on this piece will be appreciated, as that is what really takes the time. The action of the horses had to be carefully studied out, not only to be correct but also attractive. The wagon is made to scale and perfect in detail; I have made several trips to Basin, Montana, and Butte to make accurate sketches of the real old ore wagons and consulted old ore drivers about the working parts, harness, hookup, etc. Upon completion several of these drivers okayed the job, and could not find anything missing."

Plate 71. *Taking Up the Slack*, Bronze, 16¾" x 66" x 6⅞", 1981.

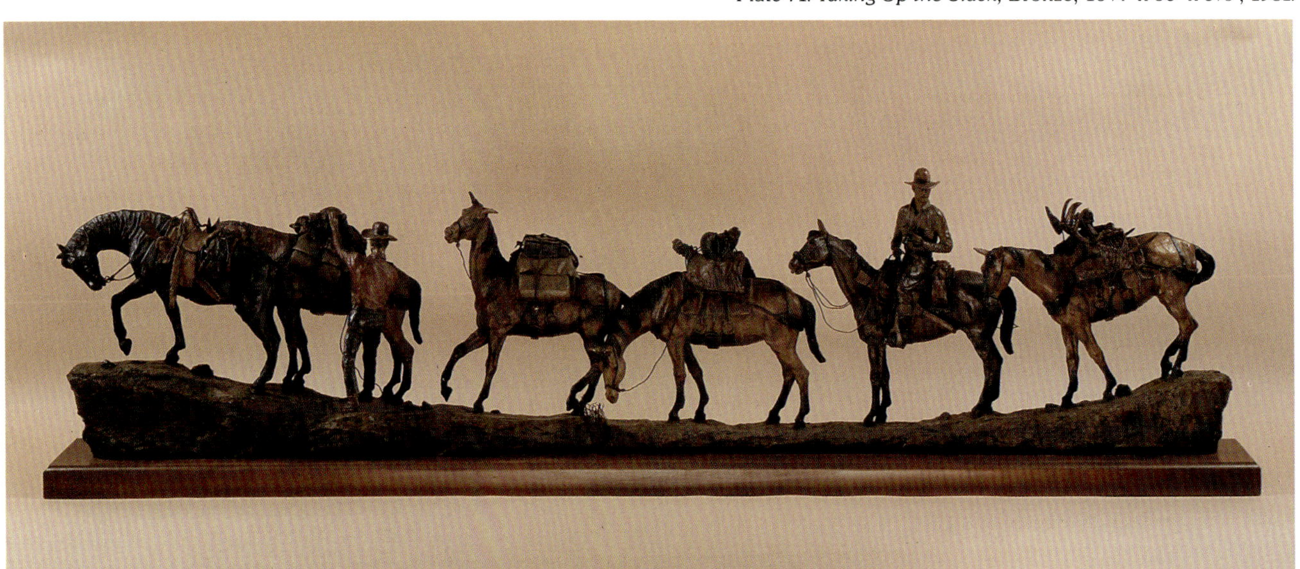

ROBERT ELMER LOUGHEED

(1910 – 1982)
b. Massie, Ontario, Canada

"We who paint horses and people are not able to sell our public a two-legged horse or a four-legged man such as a lot of modern artists do. We have to paint images that look like what they represent." – 1979

Plate 72. *Bell String on the Move,* Oil on canvas, 29¾" x 60", sight, 1974, Collection of Robert F. Rockwell, Jr.

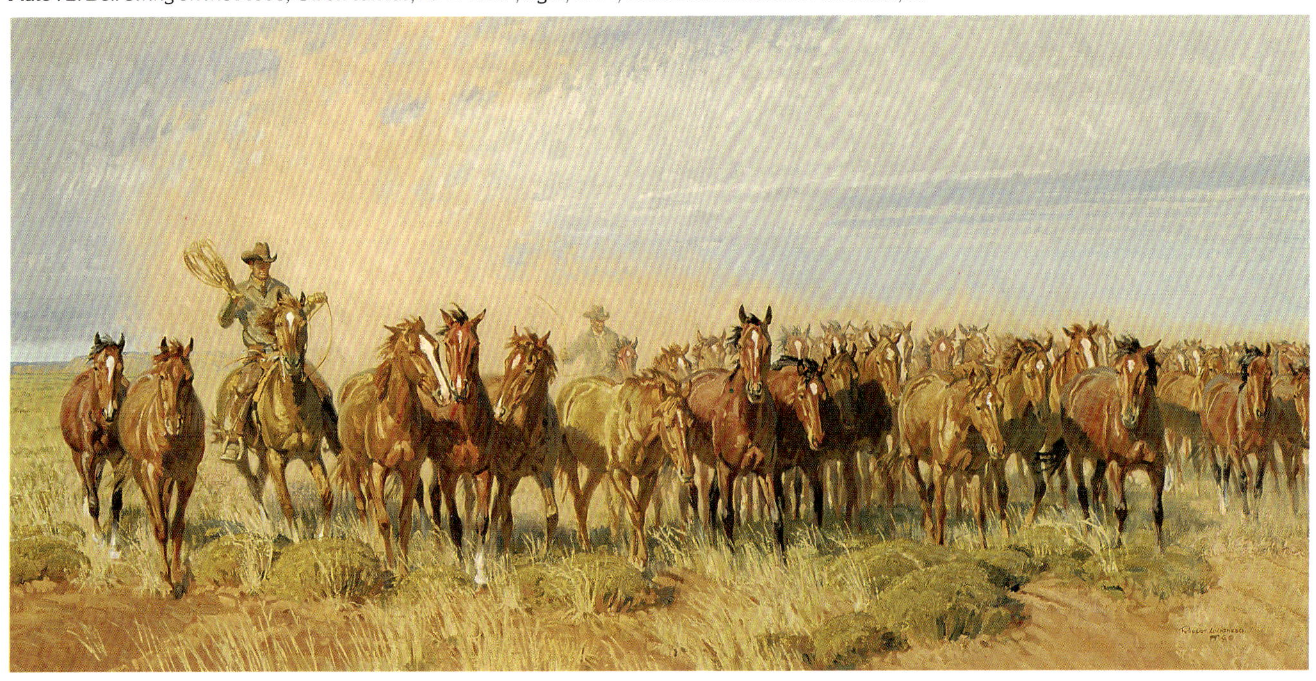

ROBERT MACFIE SCRIVER

(1914–)

b. Browning, Montana

"After analyzing art of many kinds, I have come to the conclusion that the thing that is unique about typical 'western art' is its story-telling quality. In other words, the story it tells is of more importance than design, composition, etc."

Plate 73. *Grizzly in a Trap*, Bronze, 17″ x 16″ x 17½″, 1959, Collection of Robert F. Rockwell, Jr.

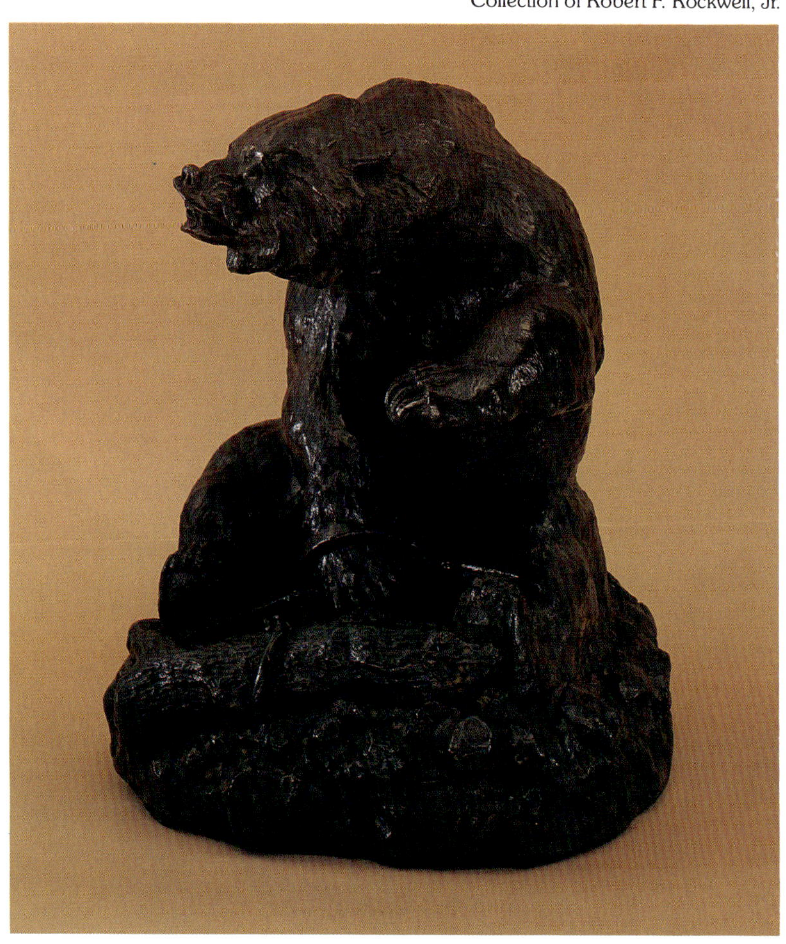

WILSON HURLEY

(1924–   )
b. Tulsa, Oklahoma

"The vertical granite face of the mile high Sandia fault lies east of Albuquerque. Great slices of the earth's crust were sheared from the uplifted mass and stand knifelike before the wall or lie in weathered foothills to the west. La Cueva Canyon cuts through them out into a pocket of loose boulders and live oak trees.

"This is a view eastward toward the mountain up La Cueva Canyon on a winter afternoon."

Plate 74. *La Cueva Cañon, Sandias,* Oil on canvas, 30″ x 48″, 1982.

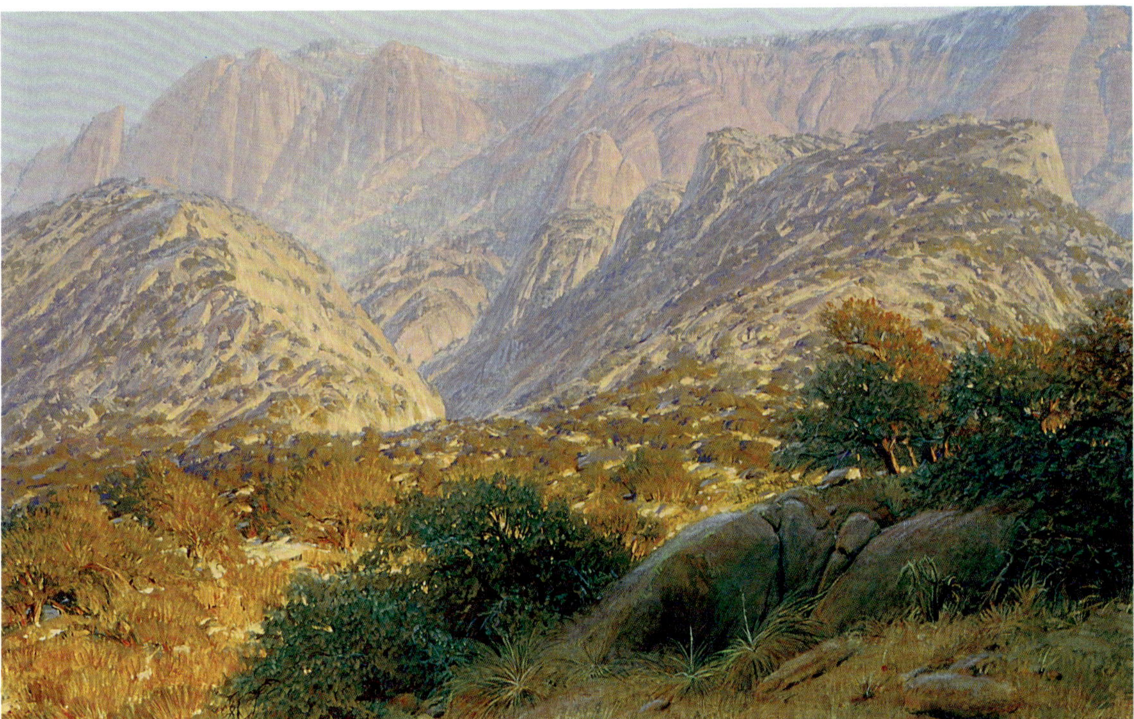

HARRY JACKSON
(1924–)
b. Chicago, Illinois

"I see this piece as the spokes of a wheel going fast. Its center is moving forward and those spokes are spinning around – some are aimed backward, some forward, some down, and some up, but that wheel is moving forward and they're all working together. My whole body sculpted that piece. It's a piece that is all rolling in the same direction."

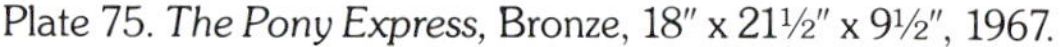
Plate 75. *The Pony Express,* Bronze, 18″ x 21½″ x 9½″, 1967.

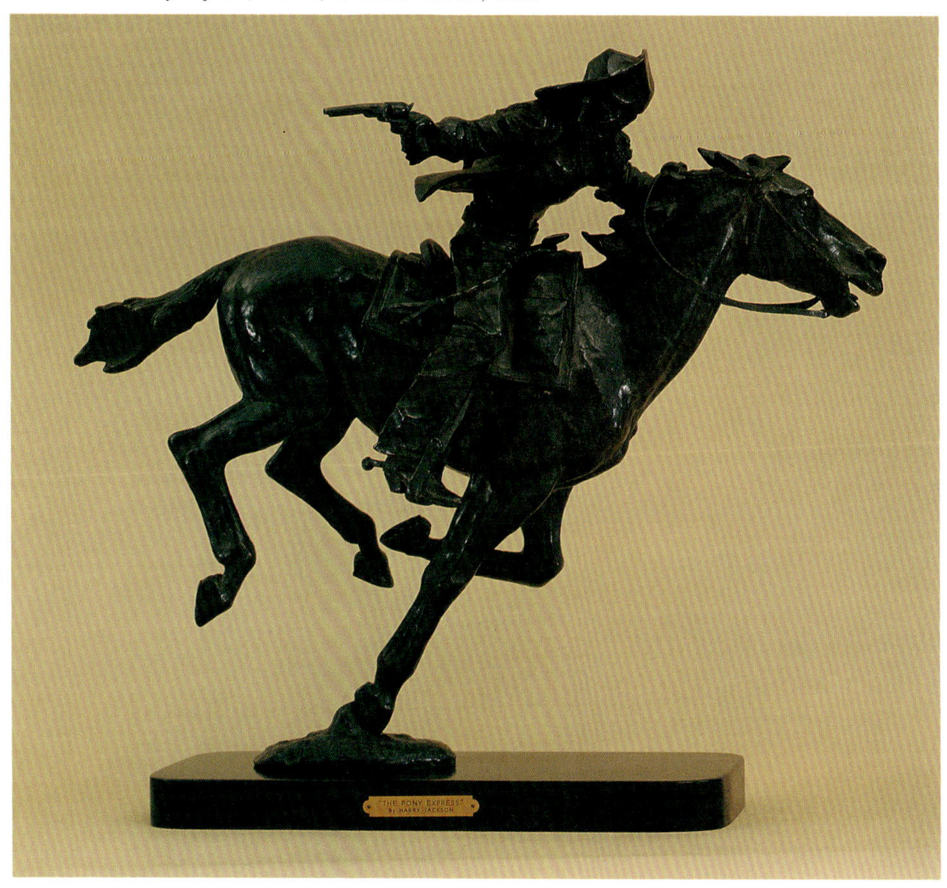

JOE NEIL BEELER

(1931 –   )
b. Joplin, Missouri

"Through truths and half-truths, legends have come forth to surround the cowboy with a maze of adventures and excitement that has caught the imagination of everyone. The by-products of the cowboy have probably produced more money than was ever made being in the cattle business". . . . – 1971

Plate 76. *Memories of Yesterday,*
Bronze, 15¾" x 15½" x 11⅝", 1979,
Gift of Katherine Smith Miller.

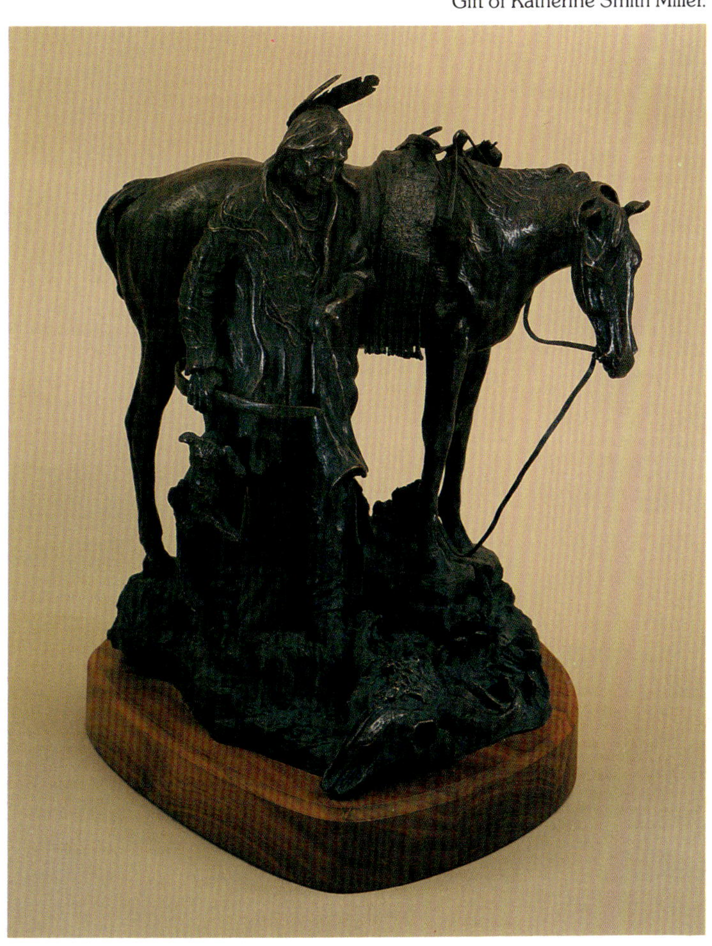

HAROLD JOE WALDRUM
(1934–)
b. Savoy, Texas

"I begin the painting with many details: the cracks in the walls, a light bulb over the door, maybe a ladder on the roof, or a drain gutter on the edge of the roof. I eliminate these things as I paint."

Plate 77. *La iglesia de San Ildefonso,* Acrylic on canvas, 54″ x 54″, 1985, Anonymous gift.

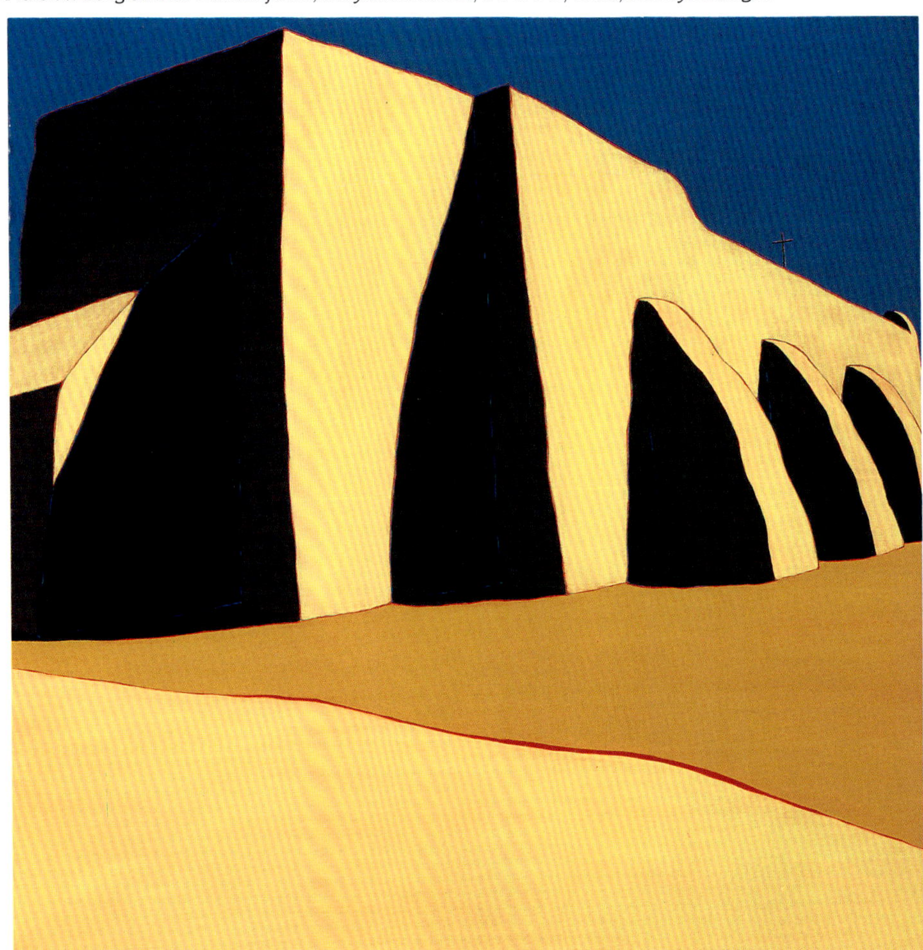

EDWARD JAMES FRAUGHTON

(1939–   )
b. Park City, Utah

"First, art is technical. It represents a reverence for the use of earth's most basic substances. Second, man and art both succeed and survive on emotional expression. The spiritual aspect of the work is every bit as important as pure craftsmanship. One without the other is out of balance. Perfection is the best of both–perfect harmony."

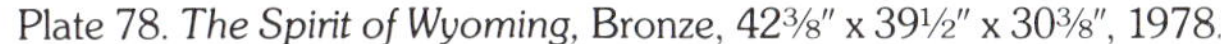

Plate 78. *The Spirit of Wyoming*, Bronze, 42⅜" x 39½" x 30⅜", 1978.

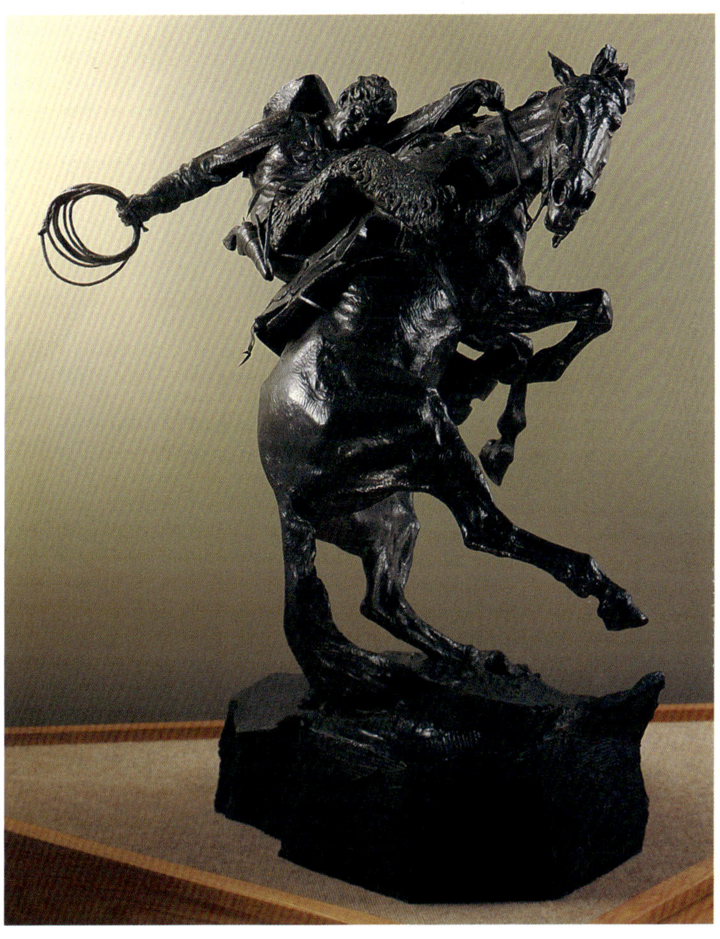

CLYDE ASPEVIG

(1951–)

b. Rudyard, Montana

"Waiting to capture the effect I want doesn't require patience. Rather, it's selfishness. I'm so keyed up, at such an intensive level when I paint. When I can make nature give me the scene I want, I feel like I've won."

Plate 79. *High Country Pond,* Oil on canvas, 32½" x 48¼", 1986.

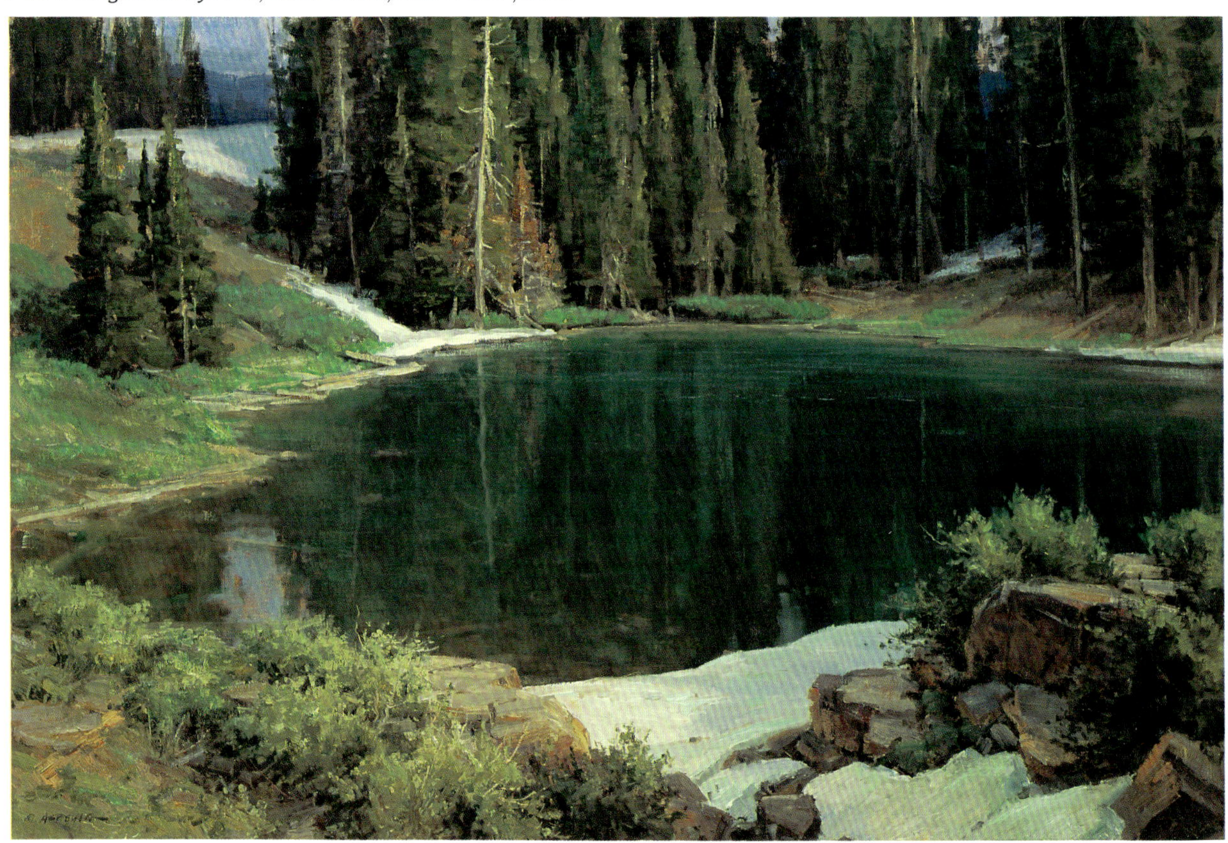

CHECKLIST

ARTIST	TITLE	DATE	MEDIUM	PLATE #
Anonymous	*Indian on Horseback*	1845	Oil	
	Mountain Landscape	1900	Oil	
Aspevig, Clyde	*High Country Pond*	1986	Oil	79
	Winter in Zion	1987	Oil	
Audubon, John James	*Ursus-Ferox, Lewis & Clark, Grizzly Bear, Males*	1848	Lithograph	
Beeler, Joe Neil	*Memories of Yesterday*	1979	Bronze sculpture	76
	Charlie Dye	1981	Bronze sculpture	
Berninghaus, Oscar Edmund	*Indians*	1920	Oil	57
	Cool Water	1950	Oil	
	In Old New Mexico	1951	Oil	
Bierstadt, Albert	*Western Landscape – Mount Rainier, Mount Saint Helens*	1863	Oil	
	Mt. Whitney	1875	Oil	11
	Yosemite Valley	1880	Oil	
	Austrian Tyrol	ca. 1855	Oil	
	Last of Fifty Million or *Buffalo* or *Buffaloes Asleep*	1863-1870	Oil	10
Bodmer, Karl	*Fort MacKenzie*	1833	Aquatint	
	Assiniboin Indians	1839	Aquatint	
	Chief of the Blood-Indians, War Chief of the Piekann Indians, Koutani Indian	1839	Aquatint	
	Dance of the Mandan Indians	N.D.	Aquatint	
	Fort Union	N.D.	Aquatint	
	Hunting of the Grizzly Bear	N.D.	Aquatint	
	Scalp Dance of the Minatarres	N.D.	Aquatint	
	Indians Hunting the Bison	ca. 1835	Aquatint	
	The Travellers Meeting with Minatarre Indians, near Fort Clark	ca. 1843	Aquatint	
Borein, John Edward	*The Stampede*	1913	Ink and gouache	
	After the Kill	1915	Wash drawing	
	Boom Town	1916	Ink and gouache	
	The Calgary Stampede	1916	Ink and gouache	54
	Wild Horse Race 1916	1916	Ink and gouache	
	Longhorns	1920	Etching and drypoint	
	The Mexican Cowboy	1920	Watercolor	
	Combing a Draw, two impressions, different states	1921	Etching and drypoint	
	Trail's End	1927	Etching	
	Trail Rider Holding the Herd	1940	Watercolor	
	Charging Hawk	N.D.	Etched copper plate	
	Crow Horse Guard	N.D.	Etched zinc plate	
	House with High Chimney	N.D.	Etched copper plate	
	House with High Chimney	N.D.	Etching and drypoint	
	Two Riders	N.D.	Pen and ink drawing	
	Thirty-eight untitled pen and ink drawings	N.D.		
	Untitled	N.D.	Etching and drypoint	
	Medicine Man and Indian Chief	ca. 1916	Ink and gouache	
	Roaring Western Frolic	ca. 1916	Ink and gouache	
	Dividing the Riders	ca. 1920	Etching and drypoint	
	Flathead Indians	ca. 1920	Etching and drypoint	

ARTIST	TITLE	DATE	MEDIUM	PLATE #
	Grass Hunters, No. 1	ca. 1920	Etching and drypoint	
	House at Laguna	ca. 1920	Etched zinc plate	
	House at Laguna	ca. 1920	Etching and drypoint	
	Mission San Juan Capistrano	ca. 1920	Etching and drypoint	
	Mission Santa Barbara, No. 1	ca. 1920	Etching and drypoint	
	On the Range	ca. 1920	Etching and drypoint	
	Out of the Mesquite	ca. 1920	Etching and drypoint	
	Roped Steer	ca. 1920	Etching and drypoint	
	Roping a Wild One	ca. 1920	Watercolor	
	Running Wild Horses	ca. 1920	Etching and drypoint	
	The Long Throw, second state	ca. 1920	Etching and drypoint	
	The Maverick	ca. 1920	Etching and drypoint	
	The Passing Herd or *Cattle and Horsemen*	ca. 1920	Watercolor	
	Three Buckaroos	ca. 1920	Watercolor	55
	Trail Boss	ca. 1920	Etching and drypoint	
	Umatilla Horse Dance	ca. 1920	Etched copper plate	
	Umatilla Horse Dance	ca. 1920	Etching and drypoint	
	Who Wins?	ca. 1920	Etching and drypoint	
	Wild Cattle, No. 2, two impressions, different states	ca. 1920	Etching and drypoint	
Bosin, F. Blackbear	*Winter Crossing* or *Ice Crossing*	1963	Gouache	
Bryers, Duane	*Hot Summer's Night*	ca. 1978	Oil	
Cary, William de la Montagne	*The Fishermen*	1870-1880	Oil	
	The Captive White Child	1875	Oil	
	The Upper Missouri	1875	Oil	14
	Indians Jousting	ca. 1875	Oil	
Cassidy, Ira Diamond Gerald	*Santiago Narranjo*	N.D.	Watercolor	
Catlin, George	*The Mandan Indians*	1871	Oil	2
	Ball-Play Dance	N.D.	Lithograph	
	Hunting Antelope	N.D.	Lithograph	
	Breaking Down the Wild Horse	ca. 1840	Oil	1
	Breaking Down the Wild Horse	ca. 1840	Pencil and wash drawing	
Chain, Mrs. James	*Black Canyon*	1896	Oil	
	Mount of the Holy Cross	1896	Oil	
Clymer, John Ford	*Time of Hunger*	1975	Oil	70
	Trouble on the River	ca. 1970	Gouache	
Coleman, Michael	*Sioux Lookout*	1976	Gouache	
Colman, Samuel	*Point Sublime—Colorado Canyon*	1892	Watercolor	
Couse, Eanger Irving	*Jonchonwit*	1897	Oil	
	Cliff Dwellers or *Early Picture Makers* or *Montezuma's Legend*	ca. 1925	Oil	46
	The Call	ca. 1925	Oil	
	The Apprentice	N.D.	Oil	45
	Tom-Tom Player—Firelight	ca. 1920	Oil	
	Makeup Time	ca. 1925	Oil	
Craig, Charles	*Indian Pueblo*	1884	Oil	
Dallin, Cyrus Edwin	*The Archery Lesson*	1907	Bronze sculpture	
de Harport, David L.	*The Old West, Bagdad Siding*	1969	Silver print photograph	
Deming, Edwin Willard	*Free Trappers*	1830	Oil	
Dorne, Albert	*Cowboy*	N.D.	Watercolor	

ARTIST	TITLE	DATE	MEDIUM	PLATE #
Dunn, Harvey T.	*Montana Winter Scene*	1914	Oil	63
	George Figured a Course from the Heavens and Found It Took Him Nowhere	1910	Oil	
Dunton, William Herbert "Buck"	*The Helping Hand*	1910	Oil	61
	Deer Hunter's Camp	1926	Oil	
	Bronco Buster	ca. 1905	Oil	
Dye, Charles R. C. "Charlie"	*Come and Get It*	1961	Oil	69
	Planning the Roundup	1961	Oil	
	Sundown for Sam Bass	1961	Oil	
Eastman, Seth	*The Tanner*	1848	Oil	3
Eggenhofer, Nick	*The Buffalo Hunt*	1960	Oil	67
	Cow Camp Colorado or *Stirrup Bar Ranch – Colorado*	1961	Oil	
	Roundup Morning	1963	Oil	
	Moving Camp	1964	Gouache	
	Bessie B, after C. M. Russell	ca. 1923	Bronze sculpture	
	In Dakota Country	ca. 1960	Oil	
Farny, Henry François	*On the Trail in Winter*	1894	Gouache	16
	The Wailer	1895	Gouache	17
	The Sign of Peace	1908	Oil	
Fraser, James Earle	*End of the Trail*	1908	Bronze sculpture	59
Fraughton, Edward James	*The Spirit of Wyoming*	1978	Bronze sculpture	78
Frenzeny, Paul	*Indian Party*	ca. 1875	Watercolor	
Gomez, Marco Antonio "Tony"	*New Home*	ca. 1955	Oil	
Goodwin, Philip Russell	*Outdoor Recreation*	ca. 1920	Oil	
Hansen, Herman Wendleborg	*Apache Scouts Trailing Government Scouts*	ca. 1915	Watercolor	
	Questionable Companions	ca. 1915	Watercolor	19
Hauser, John	*On a Hot Trail*	1903	Gouache	
	Indian Encampment	1900	Watercolor	
	On the Cheyenne	N.D.	Oil	
	Sioux Hunting Camp	ca. 1910	Oil	
	The Chief's Visit	1909	Oil	
	Chief Plenty Horses	ca. 1905	Oil	20
Heikka, Earle Erik	*Bringing in Nanooksoah*	1934	Clay model	
	Going to Town	1938	Clay model	
	Taking Up the Slack	1981	Bronze sculpture	71
	Unexpected	ca. 1939	Bronze sculpture	
Hennings, Ernest Martin	*The Teacher* or *Songs of Old*	ca. 1925	Oil	64
Hill, Thomas	*Gateway of the Yosemite Valley*	1884	Oil	
	Yosemite	N.D.	Oil	9
Holdredge, Ransom Gillet	*Indian Encampment*	N.D.	Oil	
Hurley, Wilson	*La Cueva Cañon, Sandias*	1982	Oil	74
Imhof, Joseph A.	*Taos Indian*	ca. 1950	Pastel drawing	
Jackson, Harry	*The Pony Express*	1967	Bronze sculpture	75
Johnson, Frank Tenney	*The Morning Shower*	1927	Oil	56
	Branding	ca. 1925	Oil	
Johnston, Keith	Map of the *United States of North America*	ca. 1840	Engraving	
Kauba, Carl	*The Scout*	1900	Bronze sculpture	
Kemeys, Edward	*Coyote*	ca. 1900	Bronze sculpture	15
Key, John Ross	*Mt. Diablo from the San Joaquin*	1871	Oil	

ARTIST	TITLE	DATE	MEDIUM	PLATE #
Koerner, William Henry Dethlef	*Tomahawk and Long Rifle*	1928	Oil	
	Alcalde's Welcome to Taos	1931	Oil	62
Krieghoff, Cornelius David	*The Storyteller*	1855-1860	Oil	7
Latoix, Gaspard	*Navajo*	ca. 1890	Oil	
Laurence, Sydney	*Mt. McKinley*	1922	Oil	44
Leigh, William Robinson	*The Warning Shadow*	1908	Watercolor	
	Master of His Domain	1920	Oil	
	Return of the War Canoes	1920	Oil	47
	The Great Buffalo Hunt	1947	Oil	48
Lillywhite, Raphael	*Teed and Blue Dog*	ca. 1940	Oil	65
Lion, Henry	*C. M. Russell*	ca. 1925	Bronze sculpture	
Lougheed, Robert Elmer	*Bell String on the Move*	1974	Oil	72
Marks, George B.	*The Cowboy*	1977	Bronze sculpture	
Markus, Kurt	*Bert Ancell, Bell Ranch, New Mexico 1983*	1983	Silver print photograph	
Miller, Alfred Jacob	*Pursuit*	1837	Wash and gouache	
	War Ground	1837	Wash and gouache	
	Crow Indian on Horseback	1844	Oil	5
	Crow Chief on the Lookout	ca. 1840	Oil	4
	Indian Village	ca. 1840	Oil	
	Lake Scene, Oregon	ca. 1840	Watercolor	
	Shenandoah River, Virginia	ca. 1853	Oil	
Moran, Thomas	*Crossing Green River*	1877	Oil	12
	Clouds in the Canyon	1915	Oil	13
Paxson, Edgar Samuel	*Heinmoot Tooyalaket, Chief Joseph of the Nez Perce*	1905	Watercolor	18
Phippen, George	*The Night Shift*	ca. 1961	Oil	
Pleissner, Ogden Minton	*Lost Lake, Wyoming*	1940	Oil	68
Proctor, Alexander Phimister	*The Bull Moose*	1903	Bronze sculpture	
Raschen, Henry	*Riders in the Rockies*	ca. 1920	Oil	
Remington, Frederic Sackrider	*Truce of the Indian Wars*	1886	Pen and ink drawing	
	Cutting Out a Steer	1888	Oil	26
	Heralding the Sunrise	1888	Oil	
	Stalking Goats on the Bald Peaks	1888	Oil	
	Take Off Your Boots	1888	Oil	
	The First Shot	1888	Oil	
	Splitting the Herd	1889	Ink and wash drawing	27
	Song of Hiawatha, twelve original illustrations	1890	Pen and ink drawings	
	"As the smoke lifted, he discerned the settler kneeling for a second shot"	1891	Wash and gouache	
	Indian Pack Pony	1892	Ink and wash drawing	
	Taking the Bull by the Horns	1894	Ink and wash drawing	
	The Bronco Buster, two casts	1895	Bronze sculptures	28
	Lin McLean	1887	Ink and wash drawing	29
	Old Monte	1897	Ink and wash drawing	
	"Then I jumped to my feet and told the visitors to throw off their blankets"	1900	Oil	30
	A Bunch of Buckskins, two complete sets of prints	1901	Lithographs	
	The Arizona Cowboy	1901	Pastel and pencil drawing	31
	The Cheyenne	1901	Bronze sculpture	
	The Scalp	1901	Bronze sculpture	32

ARTIST	TITLE	DATE	MEDIUM	PLATE #
	The Last Stand	1902	Photogravure	
	The Mountain Man	1903	Bronze sculpture	33
	The Sergeant	1904	Bronze sculpture	
	The Rattlesnake	1905	Bronze sculpture	34
	Paleolithic Man	1906	Bronze sculpture	
	The Outlaw	1906	Bronze sculpture	35
	The Savage	1908	Bronze sculpture	
	Winter Campaign	1909	Oil	36
	Hello Bill	N.D.	Illustrated letter	
	Letter to Whitney or *Polo Player*	N.D.	Illustrated letter	
	My Dear Gus	N.D.	Illustrated letter	
	My Dear Gus	N.D.	Illustrated letter	
	Pals	N.D.	Pen and ink drawing	
	The Life of Frederic Remington Aged 8 Years on Camp's Football Team	N.D.	Pen and ink drawing	
	Western Types, five prints	N.D.	Lithographs	
	Wild Mountain Sheep	ca. 1888	Pen and ink drawing	
	Reaction Equals Action	ca. 1890	Gouache	
Rockwell, Norman Percevel	*The Buffalo Hunt*	1915	Oil	
Rötig, Carl F.	*Buffalo Watering*	1921	Oil	
Rungius, Carl	*Mule Deer, Snow Creek, Montana*	1903	Oil	
	Alert	1905	Bronze sculpture	50
	Woodland Caribou	ca. 1914	Oil	
	Bighorn Sheep	ca. 1915	Bronze sculpture	51
	Osborne's Caribou	1926	Drypoint	
	Alaskan Wilderness	1928	Drypoint	
	#3 Goats, two impressions, different states	N.D.	Drypoint	
	Untitled	N.D.	Drypoint	
	The Challenge or *Elk*	ca. 1896	Oil	
	The Monarchs of the Wilderness	ca. 1901	Oil	49
	Elk Herd	ca. 1922	Oil	
	Rams	ca. 1925	Drypoint	
	Friends Again	ca. 1928	Drypoint	
	Old Baldface	ca. 1930	Drypoint	
	Two Moose	ca. 1930	Drypoint	
	The Stranger	ca. 1932	Oil	
	In the Bighorn Country	ca. 1943	Oil	52
Russell, Charles Marion	*Friend Bob*	1898	Illustrated letter	
	Stolen Horses	1898	Oil	37
	Chief Bear Claw	1900	Watercolor	
	A Russell Buffalo	1901	Wax and wood model	
	Bessie B.	1901	Wax and wood model	38
	A Russell Buffalo	1901; 1961	Bronze sculpture	43
	Bessie B.	1901; 1961	Bronze sculpture	39
	One Down and Two To Go	1902	Watercolor	
	Buffaloes and Wolves	1903	Watercolor	
	Chief Portrait #8	1903	Watercolor	
	Sun River War Party	1903	Oil	40
	The Forked Trail	1903	Oil	
	Cowboy	1904	Watercolor	

ARTIST	TITLE	DATE	MEDIUM	PLATE #
Russell, Charles Marion	*How Good Fren*	1907	Illustrated letter	
	The Train Robbery	1907	Pen and ink drawing	
	A Mix Up	1910	Oil	41
	Idaho Ox Teams Were Bringing In Some 6,000,000 lbs. of Freight Annually	1910	Pen and ink drawing	
	Piegan Chief	1912	Watercolor	
	The West	1913	Oil	
	Manchurian Warrior	1914	Watercolor	
	Dudes	1915	Watercolor	
	Centerfire Man Roping a Wolf or *A Cowboy Roping a Wolf*	1916	Watercolor with ink	
	A Game Country	1917	Illustrated letter	42
	I Was at the Winnepeg Stampede	1917	Illustrated letter	
	Steve Marshland Was Hanged by Vigilantes	1918	Pen and ink drawing	
	Wild Men That Parkman Knew	1921	Illustrated letter	
	Francis Parkman's *Oregon Trail* (1897), with forty-nine illustrations	1921	Watercolors	
	Curley Reaches the Far West with the Story of the Custer Fight	1922	Pen and ink drawing	
	I Never Knew a Cowman To Ware Anything But Silk	1924	Illustrated letter	
	To Noses That Read, a Smell That Spells Man	1925	Bronze sculpture	
	Coming West	1926	Illustrated letter	
	Redbird #3	1926	Clay model	
	Redbird	1926	Bronze sculpture	
	Pinto	ca. 1887	Oil	
	Bear at Lake	ca. 1888	Oil	
	Indian Head	ca. 1890	Pen and ink drawing	
	The Bear Paw Pool	ca. 1896	Illustrated letter	
	The Robe Trader	ca. 1898	Pen and ink drawing	
	So Me Run Up Behind, Shove de Gun in His Back	ca. 1899	Pen and ink drawing	
	The Initiation of the Tenderfoot	ca. 1899	Pen and ink drawing	
	Smoking Up	ca. 1903	Bronze sculpture	
	Cowboy on a Bucking Horse	ca. 1907	Pen and ink drawing	
	A Party of Sitting Bull's Braves Get on Our Trail	ca. 1922	Watercolor	
	Three Indian Warriors	ca. 1922	Watercolor	
	Here's Hoping Your Trail Is a Long One	ca. 1924	Watercolor	
Schonborn, Anton	*Fort C. F. Smith, Wy. T., Bird's-Eye View from the S. W., 1867*	1867	Pen and ink drawing	
	Fort Philip Kearney, Wy. T., Bird's Eye View from the East, 1867	1867	Pen and ink drawing	
	Fort Philip Kearney, Wy. T., Bird's Eye View from the South, 1867	1867	Pen and ink drawing	
	Fort Reno, Wy. T., 1867, Bird's Eye View from the S. W.	1867	Pen and ink drawing	
Schreyvogel, Charles	*An Unexpected Enemy*	1900	Oil	24
	Dead Sure	1902	Oil	
	The Last Drop	1903	Bronze sculpture	25
	White Eagle	N.D.	Bronze sculpture	
Scriver, Robert Macfie	*Grizzly in a Trap*	1959	Bronze sculpture	73

ARTIST	TITLE	DATE	MEDIUM	PLATE #
Seltzer, Olaf Carl Bǿrre	*Indian Squaw and Vignette*	1904	Watercolor	
	Square Butte	1912	Watercolor	
	Fool's Fire	1920	Oil	60
	Christmas card and envelope	1927	Illustrated letter	
	Dear North	1945	Illustrated letter	
	War Party or *Indian War Party*	ca. 1920	Watercolor	
Sharp, Joseph Henry	*Chief Ogalalla Fire*	1898	Oil	
	Walks the Country, Sioux	ca. 1898	Oil	
	Winter in Montana or *In Old Montana*	1903	Oil	
	Horse Runs Ahead, Sioux	ca. 1910	Oil	22
	Prayer to the Spirit of the Buffalo	ca. 1910	Oil	23
	The Ex-Governor of Taos	1910	Oil	
	The Gift Dance Drummers	1910	Oil	21
	Twilight of a Dying Race	1910	Oil	
	Crow Burial on the Little Bighorn	ca. 1910	Oil	
	Crow Grave	ca. 1910	Oil	
	Crow Reservation	ca. 1910	Oil	
	Early Campers in Montana	ca. 1910	Oil	
	Spring in Montana	ca. 1910	Oil	
	Summer in Montana	ca. 1910	Oil	
	Three Scenes or *Teepees* or *Montana Sketches*	ca. 1910	Oil	
	War Bonnet or *Old War Bonnet*	ca. 1906	Oil	
	War Chant or *The Chief's Visit* or *Bowling Deer and Hunting Son*	ca. 1910	Oil	
Shrady, Henry Merwin	*The Buffalo*	1899	Bronze sculpture	
	Elk Buffalo	1900	Bronze sculpture	53
	Moose	1901	Bronze sculpture	
	Fighting Buffalo	1903	Bronze sculpture	
Shuster, William Howard	*Pasqualita*	1928	Oil	
Stanley, John Mix	*The Smoke Signal*	1868	Oil	6
Surber, William	*Village*	1978	Watercolor	
Tait, Arthur Fitzwilliam	*Doe and Fawn*	1874	Oil	
Ufer, Walter	*Along the Rio Grande* or *New Mexican Pastime*	1920	Oil	58
van Brunt, Ted	*Pueblo Governor*	1965	Watercolor	
von Schmidt, Harold	*Rustlers at Work*	1934	Oil	66
Waldrum, Harold Joe	*La Iglesia de San Ildefonso*	1985	Acrylic	77
Wieghorst, Olaf	*Mounted Indian*	N.D.	Watercolor with ink	
	Appaloosa or *Indian on Horseback*	ca. 1950	Oil	
	Cowboy on Horse in Storm	ca. 1950	Watercolor	
	Cowboy on Horse with Lariat	ca. 1950	Watercolor with ink	
	Cowboy on Horse with Rope or *Roper*	ca. 1950	Watercolor with ink	
Wimar, Carl Ferdinand	*On the Warpath*	1860	Oil	8
Wolfe, Wayne E.	*Morning Still-String Lake*	1988	Oil	
Wright, Bill	*Rancho El Milagro, Lajitas Series*	N.D.	Silver print photograph	
	Reyes Hernandez, Big Bend Travel Park, Terlingua, Texas	N.D.	Silver print photograph	
Zogbaum, Rufus Fairchild	*Away in a Hurry*	1880	Watercolor	

THE ROCKWELL MUSEUM

ESTABLISHED IN 1976, the Rockwell-Corning Museum opened in temporary quarters in the Baron Steuben Building in Corning, New York, to display a portion of Robert and Hertha Rockwell's American western art collection. In June of 1982, following substantial support from Corning Glass Works, the Corning Glass Works Foundation, the Ingersoll-Rand Company, and community residents and friends of the Rockwells, the Rockwell Foundation's collections of American western art and artifacts, Frederick Carder glass, and turn-of-the-century toys were consolidated and installed in the old City Hall building in downtown Corning. The brick Romanesque building, constructed in 1893, was renovated and restored for that purpose, and is listed on the National Register of Historic Places. In January of 1981, the name of the museum was changed to The Rockwell Museum, and in December of 1983, the Rockwell Foundation consolidated with The Rockwell Museum, chartered under the education law of the State of New York.

The subsequent years have been spent cataloguing and conserving the objects, acquiring art by purchase and donation, organizing special exhibitions and programs that relate to the collections, completing the interpretation of the collections for visitors, and traveling objects to other museums for special exhibitions.

An annual attendance of visitors from all parts of the world includes touring school groups that participate in a comprehensive program offered by the Museum's Education Department. It organizes lectures, symposia, workshops, film and video presentations, and programs for all ages. Distinguished people in the art world are regularly invited to participate in the annual American western art symposium and to research the collections.

An active exhibition program presents four or five changing shows annually, including traveling collections from major museums and galleries whose themes complement the permanent collections, and shows of fine art and crafts that reflect the cultural fabric of the community.

Funds generated by a membership program and a Museum Shop on the premises, which features southwestern crafts, Indian jewelry, books, slides, and postcards, are used to support the activities of the growing museum. An endowment fund has been established through generous bequests and is used for acquisitions.

The Museum, located at the corner of Cedar Street and Denison Parkway, is open daily Monday through Sunday and closed on national holidays. All galleries are accessible to the handicapped.